"The League of Women Voters of California has done it again! The *Guide to California Government* is a thorough, nonpartisan, easy-to-read road map for navigating the often complicated process for voting and engaging with our government. We look forward to using this amazing resource in Rock the Vote's work engaging California's citizens."

~ *Heather Smith, President, Rock the Vote*

"The *Guide to California Government* is an excellent overview of California government with clear, easy to understand explanations of how our government works. I particularly like the use of icons to highlight key concepts and offer direction for locating additional information. This publication will be very useful for those just starting to learn about their government in citizenship classes, and for first-time voters of all ages."

~ *Randall Weaver, Program Director, Project Read Literacy*

"Who better than the League of Women Voters to explain California government to us? They themselves are great examples of how to combine grassroots groups with Sacramento lobbying to change policy!"

~ *Jan Masaoka, CEO, California Association of Nonprofits (Calnonprofits)*

"When we all contribute to an evolving paradigm – one that fosters compassionate civic engagement, deliberative dialogue and cultural humility – we build the scaffolding for an equitable society. The *Guide to California Government* is a critical resource for us to make educated decisions about how we participate in a democratic process."

~ *Emily Kinner, Executive Vice President for External Affairs, Student Senate for California Community Colleges*

"As someone who registers and mobilizes thousands of college students to engage at the polls, I look forward to utilizing the *Guide to California Government* in order to best educate college-age voters. The information is brief, relevant and easy to understand."

> ~ *Miles Jason Nevin, Executive Director, California State Student Association (CSSA)*

The *Guide to California Government*, published by the League of Women Voters of California, fills a needed gap in curriculum. It is current, easy to read and understand, yet challenging enough to require students to read it closely. The Guide is essential information for every citizen or future citizen of California. Thank you, League of Women Voters, for producing this important document.

> ~ *Marsha Ingrao, President, California Council for the Social Studies*

Guide to

California

Government

16th Edition

League of Women Voters® of California

LEAGUE OF WOMEN VOTERS®
OF CALIFORNIA

EDUCATION FUND

Guide to California Government
League of Women Voters® of California
Copyright © 2015. League of Women Voters® of California. All
rights reserved.

Published by League of Women Voters® of California Education
Fund
  1107 Ninth Street, Suite 300
  Sacramento, CA 95814
  916.442.7215

League of Women Voters®, League of Women Voters® of
California, League of Women Voters® of California Education
Fund, and Adobe are all registered trademarks of their
individual organizations.

ISBN: 978-0-9632465-2-3

Library of Congress Control Number: 2015956153

Copyright 1940, 1942, 1950, 1954, 1957, 1968, 1977, 1981, 1992
Revised 1960, 1961, 1964, 1968, 1972, 1977, 1981, 1986, 1992, 2013, 2015
by
League of Women Voters® of California

Printed in the United States of America

For volume or group sales please contact the League of Women
Voters® of California Education Fund office:
  1107 Ninth Street, Suite 300, Sacramento, California 95814
  916.442.7215
  g2cg@lwvc.org

For new information and revisions go to <cavotes.org/g2cg/>

DEDICATION

In Memory of
Kathleen Barschak Caswell
1949–1998

Kathy Caswell always voted and was very disappointed that she would not be able to do so that November 1998 because she was in the hospital, a victim of lung cancer. I received a call from an excited Kathy the Monday before Election Day asking me to bring all my voting stuff from the League to the hospital because patients were going to be allowed to cast absentee ballots. We spent that afternoon discussing all the information we had on candidates and ballot measures, as she marked her ballot. Kathy never knew the results of that election because that evening she was placed on life support. She died that Friday. But Kathy knew her vote had counted because that vote was her voice and she had let her voice be heard.

~ Rita Barschak

TABLE of CONTENTS

LIST OF FIGURES

About the
League of Women Voters California and the Education Fund

The League of Women Voters of California

The League of Women Voters (LWV), a nonpartisan political organization, encourages informed and active participation in government, works to increase understanding of major public policy issues, and influences public policy through education and advocacy.

The goal of the League of Women Voters of California (LWVC) is to empower citizens to shape better communities worldwide.

The LWV is a nonpartisan political membership organization, which

- acts after study and member agreement to achieve solutions in the public interest on key community issues at all government levels
- builds citizen participation in the democratic process
- engages communities in promoting positive solutions to public policy issues through education and advocacy

The League believes in

- respect for individuals
- the value of diversity
- the empowerment of the grassroots, both within the League and in communities
- the power of collective decision making for the common good

The League
- acts with trust, integrity and professionalism
- operates in an open and effective manner to meet the needs of those we serve, both members and the public
- takes the initiative in seeking diversity in membership
- acknowledges our heritage as we seek a path to the future

The League of Women Voters of California Education Fund

The Education Fund (LWVCEF) supports voter service and civic education activities. It is a 501(c)(3) corporation, a nonpartisan, nonprofit, educational organization, which
- builds participation in the democratic process
- studies key community issues at all government levels in an unbiased manner
- enables people to seek positive solutions to public policy issues through education and conflict management
- Find out more at <cavotes.org>

The People
Who Brought You This Book

The 16th edition of the *Guide to California Government* was brought to you by many people including:

Our talented fact checkers, writers and research team: Helen Hutchison of LWV Oakland, Sandy Wolber of LWV Los Angeles, Barbara Egbert of LWV Fremont/Newark/Union City, and the California Budget and Policy Project.

The LWVC staff: Melissa Breach, Trudy Schafer, Elizabeth Leslie, Jennifer Pae, Sharon Stone, Jenny Burger, and interns Brianna Conser and Nate Calderon.

The 2013-2015 LWVC/LWVCEF Board of Directors:

Helen Hutchison, *President, LWV Oakland*

Kathy Armstrong, *First Vice President, LWV South San Mateo County*

Joanne Leavitt, *LWVC Second Vice President, LWV Santa Monica*

Kathy Souza, *LWVCEF Second Vice President, LWV Placer County*

Ellen Wheeler, *Secretary, LWV Los Altos/Mountain View Area*

Mony Flores Bauer, *Director, LWV Oakland*

ACKNOWLEDGMENTS

Sarah Diefendorf, *Director, LWV Oakland*

Syeda Reshma Inamdar, *Director, LWV Fremont/Newark/ Union City*

Kay Ragan, *Director, LWV San Diego*

Jennifer Waggoner, *Director, LWV San Francisco*

Special thanks to the volunteer team that updated the 15th edition of the *Guide to California Government:* Suzanne Stassevitch and Adele Fasick of LWV San Francisco, and Paula Hendricks.

Special thanks to the individuals who made financial contributions to produce the 15th and 16th edition of the *Guide to California Government*: Rita Barshak, Adele Stern, Paula Hendricks, Caroline de Llamas, Suzanne Stassevitch, and John Matthews.

Introduction
How to Thrive in a Democracy

Every eligible citizen of a democracy is a voter, even those who never look at a ballot. People who don't bother to participate in an election are only fooling themselves if they think they are not voting. As the late American novelist David Foster Wallace explained, *"In reality, there is **no such thing as not voting**: you either vote by voting, or you vote by staying home and tacitly doubling the value of some Diehard's vote."*

Once we recognize that living in a democracy requires all of us to make choices that affect not only ourselves but our family and friends, as well as strangers, we can see the importance of understanding our government and how it functions. Instead of passively watching what is going on in our community and then complaining about it, we can actively shape the future by choosing candidates who share our principles, letting them know what direction we want them to take, and holding them accountable for the way they manage the people's business. The key to shaping the community you live in is to do these things:

- Vote.
- Let your representatives know what you want them to do.
- Work with others to ensure change for the better.
- Help young people and newcomers to become active participants in governing.

The League of Women Voters® of California has prepared this guide to help you find your way through the complicated tangle of state government. The guide starts, as all democratic governance starts, with voting and elections then moves on to describe other important aspects of government:

- separating the powers of the legislative, the executive, and the judicial branches
- working with other levels of government
- paying for government
- providing public education
- understanding how California's government developed

HOW TO USE THIS GUIDE

To make it easier for you to zoom in on the information you really want to know, we have used icons in the margins to highlight particular types of information. Look for these symbols:

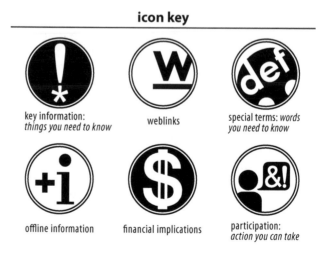

icon key

key information: *things you need to know*

weblinks

special terms: *words you need to know*

offline information

financial implications

participation: *action you can take*

Whenever possible we have included the relevant websites for government officials, departments and agencies. URLs are separated from the text by angle brackets; for example <ca.gov/>.

While we have tried to provide definitions and explanations in the text of the book, we have also provided in the Appendix some important lists: abbreviations and acronyms; state constitutional officials; salaries of elected officials; and regional associations of governments. Many industries and organizations have their own ways of talking about things, their own jargon, so we have included a section called "The Language of Government." We hope you find this useful.

We have tried to make this guide as accurate as possible and have presented information current as of Sept 2015. We have also included a URL for each of the relevant websites; most of these are government sources that contain the most up-to-date information on the topics covered. It is always a good idea to check the agency or department website when you use specific information found in this publication. Government data changes quickly and often unexpectedly.

This guide offers only a brief outline of how government works in California, but our hope is that it will give you a start on the lifelong challenge of living in a democracy. As the League of Women Voters has proclaimed for years, "*Democracy is not a spectator sport.*" Now is the time for all of us to become active.

Exercising Citizen Rights

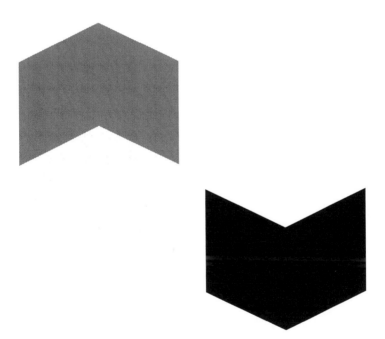

PART I

Voters and Elections

<www.sos.ca.gov/elections>

Free elections are the foundation of a democracy and the most important element in an election is the voters. The constitutions of both the United States and California specifically protect the right to vote. In California there are five basic factors that determine who can vote.

WHO MAY VOTE?

People can vote if they
- are United States citizens
- are at least 18 years of age or will be on the date of the election
- live in California
- are registered to vote 15 days prior to election day

In 1972, the national voting age was lowered from 21 to 18.

Some people who meet these requirements still cannot vote:
- Persons who have been legally declared mentally incompetent cannot vote.
- Convicted felons cannot vote while they are in prison or on parole. After parole is finished, they can vote.

For further information about the right of inmates to vote, see the Secretary of State's site <http://www.sos.ca.gov/elections/voting-resources/new-voters/who-can-vote-california/voting-rights-californians/>.

A few people have special requirements for voting:
- New state residents can vote for president and vice president of the United States but not for state or local candidates. They should register at least seven days before the election.
- A voter who has recently moved to a new precinct can use a vote-by-mail ballot, vote a provisional ballot at the new precinct, or go back to the old precinct and vote there in person. Homeless people can register and vote if they can give a cross street where they are located and an address at which they can pick up mail.

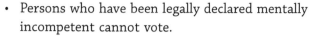

HOW CAN I REGISTER TO VOTE?

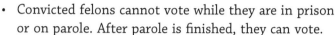

As of November 2015, the DMV plans to offer automated voter registration according to a New Motor Voter Law, AB 1461.

1. Register online at <registertovote.ca.gov/>.
   a. If your information is found in the Department of Motor Vehicles (DMV) database for your California driver license or identification card number, you can authorize elections officials' use of your DMV signature. Then an electronic image of your DMV signature will be added to your voter registration application after you click "submit" at the end of the online application.

b. If there is no signature on file with the DMV, you will need to
- enter your date of birth and last four digits of your social security number
- click "print"
- sign the paper application
- mail it to your county elections official

2. Call 800.345.VOTE (800.345.8683) and ask to have a voter registration form sent to your home.
3. Pick up an official registration postcard at your county elections office, any DMV office, or a library, post office, or other government office.

No printer? You can still register online and your county elections official will mail you a form to sign.

Follow directions on the registration form and return it to the county elections office where you live. California has permanent voter registration.

If time permits, your county elections official will contact you when your voter registration application is approved or when more information is needed to confirm your eligibility.

You must reregister only if you move or change your name or wish to change party affiliation.

A voter can register as a member of a political party (Republican, Democratic, Green, etc.) or may choose not to state a party preference. Your choice of registering as a party member or as a no-party-preference voter will affect the way you will vote in some primary elections. There is more information about primary elections in Chapter 2.

Just over 61 percent of votes cast in the November 2014 election were vote-by-mail.

VOTING BY MAIL

Voting by mail is a popular option in California. In the November 2014 election, 61 percent of the ballots cast were vote-by-mail ballots.

Any voter can register as a permanent vote-by-mail voter or can request a vote-by-mail ballot for an election. Requests must be made at least seven days before the election. Ballots are mailed 7 to 29 days before the election to voters who request them. They may be returned by mail or in person. A completed ballot may be turned in at any polling place in the county on Election Day. Vote-by-mail ballots must be postmarked on or before Election Day and received in the elections office no later than three days after Election Day.

Did you vote by mail? Make your vote count! Sign your ballot envelope.

If a voter is unable to get to the polls because of a last minute emergency, he or she can get a vote-by-mail ballot up until Election Day. An authorized person may pick up a ballot for someone confined to home or hospital and return it before the polls close.

A vote-by-mail ballot is a secret ballot and must be placed in a sealed envelope **signed by the voter**. The signature must be verified by election officials.

ELECTIONS

California citizens vote for state and federal officials in primary and general elections. They also choose local officials in local elections, which are not always held on the same day as statewide elections.

In 2010 voters approved Proposition 14, which created an open primary election system. Under this system, all candidates running for state offices in a primary election (with the exception of the Superintendent of Public Education, a non-partisan office) appear on a single primary ballot, regardless of their party preference. A voter can vote for any candidate. The top two overall vote-getters—not the top vote-getter from each political party— move to the general election. In addition, candidates are no longer allowed to run as "independents" or "write-ins" at the general election. <http://www.sos.ca.gov/elections/primary-elections-california/>.

What does that mean?

Partisan offices are those for which the candidates are nominated by a political party, such as the Democratic, Republican, or American Independent party. Partisan offices are now limited to the U.S. President and members of county and state central committees.

Voter-nominated offices are those nominated in the open primary election; these include members of the U.S. Senate and House of Representatives, California state officers, and state senators and Assembly members.

Nonpartisan offices are those for which candidates are nominated without regard to party. The party affiliation of candidates is not listed. These include the Superintendent of Education as well as judges and justices.

There are now three types of offices in California elections: partisan, voter-nominated and nonpartisan.

See Figure 1.1, Federal and State Officials elected by California Voters.

More people are voting now in California than did a century ago. The turnout in November 1912 was 45 percent of 1,569,000 voters. In November 2012, the turnout was 55 percent of 23,802,577 eligible voters.

BALLOT MEASURES

In addition to the names of candidates, California ballots usually include several ballot measures.

The state Constitution requires a vote of the people on any general obligation bond act or proposal to change the Constitution. These measures must receive a two-thirds vote in each house of the Legislature before they are placed on the ballot.

In addition to propositions initiated by the Legislature, initiatives and referendums may appear on the ballot by direct action of the people. Sponsors of the measure must collect a specific number of signatures of California voters before a measure is placed on the ballot. For more information see Chapter 3.

A majority vote (50 percent plus 1 of ballots cast) is required for passage of all state ballot measures. Unless the measure itself provides otherwise, a newly-passed measure goes into effect the day after the election.

What does that mean?

California ballot measures (numbered Propositions on the ballot) have been a part of the California Constitution since 1911. They were adopted as a tool to allow citizens to propose laws and constitutional amendments without the support of the governor or the Legislature. This package of voter rights included the ability to recall elected officials, the right to repeal laws by referendum, and the ability to enact state laws by initiative. Generally, any matter that is a proper subject of legislation can become an initiative measure.

More information about ballot measures can be found on the Secretary of State's website: sos.ca.gov/elections/ballot-measures.

Local ballot measures often have different requirements from state measures. Local regulations are available from county election officers.

In cities, counties, and school districts, a majority vote is required to pass most local ballot measures and charter changes; however, all local bond measures and many local tax measures require a vote greater than a majority.

Figure 1.1 **CA Elections: Federal & State Offices**

	ELECTION	YEAR	TERM
FEDERAL OFFICE: PARTISAN			
President	statewide	years divisible by four	4 years
FEDERAL OFFICES: VOTER-NOMINATED			
U.S. Senators	statewide	every six years from 1992	6 years
		every six years from 1994	
U.S. Representatives	district	even-numbered years	2 years
STATE OFFICES: VOTER-NOMINATED			
Governor			
Lieutenant Governor			
Secretary of State			
Controller	statewide	even-numbered years when there is no presidential election	4 years
Treasurer			
Attorney General			
Insurance Commissioner			
Members of Board of Equalization	district	same as governor	4 years
State Senators	district	same as governor for even-numbered districts	4 years
		same as president for odd-numbered districts	
Assembly Members	district	even-numbered years	2 years
STATE OFFICES: NONPARTISAN			
Superintendent of Public Instruction	statewide	same as governor	4 years
Supreme Court justices	statewide	same as governor	12 years
Court of Appeal justices	statewide	same as governor	12 years
Superior Court judges	county	even-numbered years	6 years

ELECTION OFFICIALS

Find my county election officials: <http://www.sos.ca.gov/elections/voting-resources/new-voters/county-elections-offices/>.

State Level – the California Secretary of State is the chief elections officer of California.

County Level – each county has its own election officials. The structure varies by county. Some examples are:

- The county board of supervisors serves as a board of election commissioners.
- County clerk oversees the election process.
- Counties with a large population have a separate department of elections.

Local Level – each county is divided into precincts, small voting districts each of which has a polling place. The county election official creates the precincts and changes boundaries as population changes. On Election Day, each precinct is administered by a precinct board selected by the county to

- staff the polls on Election Day
- check that each person who votes is registered
- maintain security of the ballots and voting machines
- deliver completed ballots to the county election official
- provide bilingual assistance at polling places where it is required

You Can Be a Poll Worker – If you are a registered voter, or an eligible high school student, you can promote democracy in your community, earn extra money (amount varies by county) and assist voters. Contact your county elections official to apply to be a poll worker. For more information: <http://www.sos.ca.gov/elections/poll-worker-information/>.

INFORMATION FOR VOTERS

Before an election, the Secretary of State compiles a ballot pamphlet containing:

- the complete text of all proposed constitutional amendments, bond measures, initiatives and referendums
- a copy of any provisions currently in force that would be amended by the proposals
- the legislative analyst's summary of the proposals and their fiscal effects
- arguments for and against each measure, and rebuttals. The initiator of each measure usually writes the pro argument; the Secretary of State selects a con argument from among those submitted by citizen groups and individuals.

Find the ballot for your precinct at <smartvoter.org/>.

Before the pamphlet is printed and mailed, it is available for public examination in Sacramento and online at the Secretary of State's website. Any voter may challenge the accuracy and request corrections.

The ballot pamphlet is mailed to each registered voter's household 60 days before the election. County clerks send the pamphlet to voters who register later.

At the county level, the clerk/registrar compiles ballot pamphlets and sample ballots and distributes them. Each voter receives voting information on local candidates and measures that are on the ballot in his or her precinct. Arguments for and against any local measure are solicited by the clerk/registrar. In county elections, preference must be given to arguments submitted by members of the board of supervisors. Next preference is given to arguments by groups formed specifically to support or oppose the measure, followed by arguments of citizen associations. Arguments of individual citizens are chosen last. Candidates' statements, printed at their expense, may be included in local pamphlets.

ELECTION DAY

In 1911, women in California gained full voting rights.

Election Day practices are designed to encourage voting, to protect against fraud, and to ensure that no vote is invalidated because the voter doesn't understand the rules.

Poll regulations:

- Polls open at 7 AM and close at 8 PM. Anyone who is waiting in line when polls close may vote after 8 PM. Some counties may offer early voting.
- When a voting machine is used, an election official must offer to instruct the voter on its use. Counties can choose different machines from a list certified by the Secretary of State.
- Booths may not be occupied by more than one adult at a time, except for persons assisting voters with disabilities.
- A voter who spoils a ballot by making an error may return it and receive another. A voter who spoils a ballot may get two ballots in addition to the original, but no more than three.
- Spoiled ballots are cancelled by election officials and returned with the unused ballots; the election board must account for every ballot delivered to it.
- Each polling place is required to have at least one voting machine that permits voters, including those who are blind or visually impaired, to cast a ballot without assistance.

See Voter ID information on next page

Provisional Voting. California has had statutes for providing provisional ballots since 1984

- to ensure that no properly registered voter is denied the right to vote even if that voter's name is not on a

precinct's voter roll
- to help election officials ensure that no voter votes twice either intentionally or inadvertently

Challenges. A voter may be challenged on the basis of
- not being the person registered
- having already voted
- not being a resident of the district
- not being a U.S. citizen
- being a convicted felon on parole

Only a member of the precinct board may challenge a voter, although any voter may ask a board member to challenge another voter for one of the reasons listed above. The challenged voter is allowed to vote only after satisfactorily answering certain questions under oath. Any doubt in the interpretation of the law is resolved in favor of the challenged voter.

Voter Identification (ID)

Most California voters **are not required** to show identification before casting ballots; however –
- if you are voting for the first time in a federal election and you registered by mail you are required to show ID
- if you did not provide your driver license number, California identification number, or the last four digits of your social security number on the registration card when registering by mail, you may be asked to show a form of identification when you go to the polls

If you are in either of these situations, make sure you bring identification with you to the polls or include a copy of it with your vote-by-mail ballot. Following is a partial list of the more than 30 acceptable forms of identification. You can also visit the Secretary of State's website and look for "Help America Vote Act Identification Standards" at <http://www.sos.ca.gov/administration/regulations/current-regulations/elections/help-america-vote-act-identification-standards>.

- driver license or state-issued ID card
- passport
- employee ID card
- credit or debit card
- student ID
- military ID

Determining Who Has Voted. The precinct board must post outside the polling place an index of persons registered to vote in that precinct, listing voter's name, address, and party affiliation. Throughout the day, precinct officials cross off the names of those who have voted. Supporters or opponents of candidates or ballot measures may check the index and remind those who have not voted to come to the polls.

Illegal Activities. Bribery, intimidation and defrauding of voters; voting when not entitled to; tampering with voting equipment; and altering election returns are all illegal activities. The law forbids anyone within 100 feet of a polling place from electioneering or speaking to a voter about his or her vote.

Counting Ballots. Secrecy is protected for voters when they cast their ballots, but openness is emphasized when ballots are counted. Procedures have changed over the years and vary in different precincts depending on which voting machines are used and whether votes are counted at a central location. No matter what method is used, each step of the process is prescribed by law, and every step must be taken in public view of official observers. Any voter may be present at the counting but may not interfere. Vote by mail ballots are counted at the office of the county elections official. Any election may be contested and a recount requested.

TYPES OF ELECTIONS

California has three general types of elections – primary, general and local. In addition, "special elections" can be called. A special election must be held for a specific purpose, for example filling a vacancy.

Primary Elections. There are two types of primary elections:

1. In a **presidential primary** election, voters registered with a political party select the candidate who will represent that party on the ballot in the next general election in November. In most cases, individuals can only vote in the primary election of the party in which they are registered. Sometimes a political party will allow voters who have registered as "No Party Preference" to vote in its partisan primary.

2. In the **state primary**, for candidates running for U.S. congressional, state constitutional, and state offices, California now has a Top Two Open Primary system. All candidates are listed on a single statewide primary election ballot. Voters can vote for the candidate of their choice from any political party. The two candidates who receive the most votes for each office will advance to the general election in November.

   The statewide primary is held in June of even-numbered years on the first Tuesday after the first Monday. The California Legislature sets the presidential primary date. It has usually been held on the same date as the statewide primary. For further information: <cavotes. org/vote/elections/types>.

General Elections. General elections are held on the first Tuesday after the first Monday in November in even-numbered years. Each registered voter gets a ballot listing all of the candidates for each office, all of the ballot measures, and the candidates for nonpartisan offices.

Special Elections. Special elections are called when a vacancy must be filled (usually because of the death or resignation of an office holder), a recall voted on, or a decision that must be made earlier than the next regular election. To save money, special elections are often held at the same time as regularly scheduled elections.

The governor may call a special election to fill a vacancy or to determine a statewide issue, but not for bond measures; those must be approved at a regular election.

An election to fill a vacancy must be held between 112–119 days after calling the election. A primary for a special election is held on the eighth Tuesday before the election. A candidate who receives more than 50 percent of the vote wins. If no candidate

Requirements for State Recall Petitions and Replacement Candidates

A petition to recall a statewide official must be signed by voters equal to 12 percent of the total vote for that office in the most recent election. These signatures must include signatures from five different counties equal to 1 percent of the vote in that county.

A petition to recall a state legislator, judge, or member of the Board of Equalization must have signatures equal to 20 percent of the last vote for that office.

Recall proponents have 160 days in which to file the signed petitions.

The governor must call an election to be held between 60 and 80 days after the Secretary of State certifies that enough signatures have been collected.

A candidate who wishes to replace a recalled official must file a declaration of candidacy 59 days or more before the election. The person subject to the recall may not be a candidate in the replacement election.

gets 50 percent, the two with the highest votes compete in a runoff election.

Recall Elections. The state Constitution specifies two steps to be taken to remove any state or local elected official from office:

1. Circulate a petition asking for signatures from people qualified to vote for that office. The recall petition states the reasons for the recall; the officeholder need not have violated the law.

2. Hold an election to decide whether the officeholder should be removed and, if so, who shall take the position.

If the majority votes in favor of a recall, the officer is removed and the candidate receiving the most votes becomes the successor. A vacancy created by the recall of a judge is filled by the governor, or for the justice court, by the board of supervisors.

In California the recall process has been used mostly at the local level. Procedures similar to those outlined above govern the recall of officers in counties, cities and special districts.

Australia, Belgium, Greece, and several other countries have compulsory voting. People who do not vote pay a small fine or face some other sanction.

Choosing the Candidates You Vote For

<www.sos.ca.gov/elections>

The choice of which candidate to vote for is the major decision facing voters everywhere. In California, voters directly select all legislative officers. By directly electing executive officers, voters determine who will appoint other policy-making officials. For most elections, political parties recruit candidates, raise money to support campaigns, and encourage citizens to vote for their candidates. California law sets qualifications and regulates campaign expenditures of candidates; it also regulates the structure and functions of political parties.

LEGAL REQUIREMENTS FOR CANDIDATES

United States President
Every candidate shall be a natural-born citizen of the United States, at least 35 years of age, and be a resident of the United States for at least 14 years.

United States Senate

Every candidate shall be at least 30 years of age, a U.S. citizen for nine years, and a resident of California on the date he or she would be sworn into office if elected.

United States House of Representatives

Every candidate shall be at least 25 years of age, a U.S. citizen for seven years, and a resident of California on the date he or she would be sworn into office if elected.

California Governor

The California Constitution specifies that the governor must
- be a citizen of the United States and a resident of California
- be registered and qualified to vote for the office at the time the nomination papers are issued to the person*
- not served two terms in the office sought since November 6, 1990.

*Article V, section 2 of the California Constitution require five-year residency in California; however, it is the legal opinion of the Secretary of State's office that this provision violates the U.S. Constitution. (10/27/09)

California State Senate and State Assembly

Every candidate shall
- be a U.S. citizen
- be a registered voter and otherwise qualified to vote for that office at the time nomination papers are issued to the person
- not have been convicted of a felony involving bribes,

the embezzlement of public money, perjury, or con-
spiracy to commit any of those crimes

- be regulated by term limits if elected in 2012 and
after limited to 6 terms (12 years)

GETTING ON THE BALLOT

Any individual who intends to be a candidate for an elective
state office must file a Candidate Intention Statement for the
specific state office sought and provide information about
funds to be used in the campaign, including personal funds
and contributions.

A candidate must pay a filing fee, or submit signatures in lieu
of the fee. The number of signatures required varies according
to the office.

Candidates may state their political party membership or
may run as "no party preference" or as independent candidates.

Candidates for local offices follow the same rules, but filing
fees and the number of signatures required are lower than for
state offices.

Candidates in **primary** elections may run as write-in
candidates by gathering signatures to obtain nomination
papers. Because of the rules set by the Top Two Open Primary
Act (see Chapter 1, page 10) no write-in candidates may run in
the general election.

> *All of the candidates running for a voter-nominated*
> *office, regardless of political affiliation, appear on the*
> *primary ballot for each voter.*

See information box on Primary Elections on the next page.

Prop 28, passed by the voters in June 2010, reduced the total number of years a politician can serve in the Legislature from 14 to 12 years.

California's Top Two Open Primary System

1. **Primary elections.** There are two types of **primary elections.** In a presidential primary election, voters registered with a political party select the candidate who will represent that party on the ballot in the next general election in November. In most cases, individuals can only vote in the primary election of the party in which they are registered. Sometimes a political party will allow voters who have registered as "No Party Preference" to vote in their partisan primary.

2. In the **state primary,** for candidates running for U.S. congressional, and state elective offices, California now has a Top Two Open Primary system. All candidates are listed on a single statewide primary election ballot. Voters can vote for the candidate of their choice from any political party. The two candidates who receive the most votes for each office will advance to the general election in November.

CAMPAIGN FINANCING

Campaign financing is a major concern of any candidate for public office and has become a major concern to voters too. Most of the money to pay for candidates' TV, radio and Internet ads, mailing pieces, websites, and travel expenses, come from donations by individuals, corporations, unions, or other organizations.

The cost of campaigning for elective office in California has drastically increased; in recent years more than $160 million has been spent by a single candidate for a statewide office. During the 2010 gubernatorial election, candidates spent more than $250 million. The median cost of a 2012 state Senate race was $1,500,000 and the median cost of a state Assembly race was $1,000,000. By comparison, the candidates for governor in 2002 spent $118 million and the average cost of a state Senate race was under a million dollars. For more information: followthemoney.org/.

Voters overwhelmingly passed the California Political Reform Act of 1974, which requires that *"receipts and expenditures in election campaigns should be fully and truthfully disclosed in order that the voters may be fully informed,"* and that *"activities of lobbyists should be regulated and their finances disclosed ..."* This Act created the *California Fair Political Practices Commission.* One of the duties of the commission is to regulate campaign financing, contributions and spending, through regulations and oversight. Visit the commission's website to see reports on the latest election spending at fppc.ca.gov/.

You can also access and track information about campaign financing activity statewide at the Cal-Access website, cal-access.sos.ca.gov/.

THE WAY CAMPAIGN FINANCING WORKS NOW

Candidates for a state office and committees that make contributions to state candidates are subject to contribution limits from a single source for each election. The limits for 2013-2014 are shown in the table below: <fppc.ca.gov/index.php?id=446>.

Figure 2.1   Campaign Contribution Limits

CONTRIBUTOR	OFFICE ELECTION		
	SENATE & ASSEMBLY	**STATEWIDE, NOT GOVERNOR**	**GOVERNOR**
individual	$4,100	$6,800	$27,200
small contributor committee	$8,200	$13,600	$27,200
political party	no limit	no limit	no limit

Regulations governing the financing of state elections:

- **Tax deduction.** California personal income tax law allows a deduction of $100 per person for contributions to candidates in a primary or general election; also allows up to $25 of an income tax refund to be directed to a political party.
- **Reports of contributions.** Any committee that receives or spends $1,000 in a year to support or oppose a candidate or ballot measure must file a statement of organization with the Secretary of State. Candidates must also file forms stating their intention to receive or to solicit campaign funds.
- **Bank accounts.** All candidates must have a separate bank account for any campaign. Each committee's treasurer is accountable for its contributions and expenditures. A candidate must file a statement if any money, including the candidate's personal funds, is received or spent. A candidate may not use campaign funds for personal use.
- **Timing of reports.** Candidates must file a report of contributions and expenditures at least three times during an election period. Campaign committees for a candidate or for a ballot measure must file campaign disclosure statements twice during the election and once afterward.
- **Amount of contribution.** Each contribution of $100 or more in money, goods, or services must be listed with the name, address, occupation, and employer of the contributor. All expenditures of $100 or more must be itemized. Contributions or expenditures of $100 or more may not be made in cash. Anonymous contributions over $100 are prohibited.

- **Audits.** The Franchise Tax Board is required to audit all reports of all statewide and Board of Equalization candidates and candidates for the Supreme Court and Courts of Appeal who have raised or spent at least $25,000. A Political Action Committee (PACs) is also subject to audits.

The 2010 Citizens United decision of the United States Supreme Court (558 U.S. 310 (2010)) has made it possible for candidates and parties to receive large amounts of money from corporations and organizations. It is not yet clear how this decision will affect campaign financing in the future.

Conflict of Interest Rules

Public officials are not allowed to participate in governmental decisions in which they have a financial interest.

To ensure that they do not, a series of conflict of interest rules have been put in place:

- **Definition of financial interest.** An official is considered to have a financial interest if he or she has a direct or indirect interest worth more than $1,000 in a business or real property, is an officer or employee in a business, or receives income of more than $250 from an affected party within 12 months before a decision is made.

- **Who is covered by rules?** Conflict of interest provisions apply to all elected officials at all levels of government and to many high level appointees, such as senior university officials, city managers, district attorneys, judges, and members of some boards and commissions. Staff members of elected officials may also be subject to conflict of interest provisions.

- **Disclosure statements.** A candidate must file a financial disclosure statement with the original declaration of candidacy. Officeholders must file a statement within 30 days after assuming office and annually thereafter. These statements describe the nature of investments, value of real property, and income including gifts.

- **Gifts.** Elected state officers are not allowed to accept gifts with a value of more than $250 from a single source in a calendar year nor accept any honorarium. Elected local officers may not accept gifts or honoraria whose aggregate total is more than $1,000 from a single source in a calendar year. Honorarium is defined as, "any payment made in consideration for any speech given, article published, or attendance at any public or private conference, convention, meeting, social gathering, meal, or like gathering."

- **Enforcement.** The Fair Political Practices Commission (FPPC) administers and enforces the Political Reform Act. It can investigate charges of violations, subpoena records and witnesses, issue cease and desist orders, and levy fines. The commission is a five-member board, no more than three of whom may be from the same political party. The governor appoints two members from different parties; the attorney general, the Secretary of State, and the state controller each appoint one member.

- **Penalties.** Violations of the Political Reform Act may result in civil or criminal penalties. Private citizens may report violations and bring actions to stop them. Anyone convicted of a misdemeanor under the Political Reform Act may not be a candidate for office or a lobbyist for four years, unless the court rules otherwise at the time of sentencing. The criminal penalty for illegal contributions or improper reporting is a fine of up to $10,000, or three times the amount involved in the violation, whichever is greater. The attorney general enforces the criminal provisions on the state level; city attorneys and district attorneys share responsibility with the attorney general at the local level. The Fair Political Practices Commission, city attorneys, and district attorneys share responsibility for civil prosecutions. The FPPC can also levy administrative fines of up to $2,000.

CALIFORNIA'S POLITICAL PARTIES

Forming a Political Party

A political party is a public organization of citizens working to advance its governmental policies by recruiting candidates for office and waging campaigns on their behalf. A group or organization may qualify as a political party and have the names of its candidates printed on the official ballot by demonstrating popular support in one of two ways:

- The number of voters registered with that party must equal or exceed 1 percent of the votes cast in the last election for governor.
- Registered voters equal to 10 percent of those voting in the last election for governor must sign a petition declaring that they represent a political party.

The two largest political parties in California are the Democratic and Republican parties. In addition to these, the American Independent, Green, Libertarian, and Peace and Freedom parties qualified for the 2012 California ballot. In order to remain an official party, both of the following conditions must be met:

- One of the party's candidates for statewide office must have received at least 2 percent of the vote cast for that office in the last election for governor.
- The number of voters registered with that party must be at least one-fifteenth of one percent of the total state registration.

Party Organization

Who is a party member? Anyone who declares a party preference when registering to vote is legally a party member.

Americans Elect qualified as a political party in 2012 when more than 10 percent of those voting in the 2010 election for governor signed a petition declaring Americans Elect a political party.

They turned in 1,093,000 petition signatures.

10 percent of the votes cast in the 2010 election for governor was 1,009,518.

Almost 80 percent of California voters belong to a political party. (In the 2012 fall election, 21.3 percent of voters registered with no party preference.) People who want to be more active in the party may petition to be nominated to run for a position on the county or state central committee.

What is a county central committee? The county central committee organizes campaigns for party candidates in the county. Any registered party member may file a petition asking to be nominated to the committee. Members are elected at the primary election for two-year terms; vacancies are usually filled by appointment. In addition to elected members, party incumbents and nominees from that county are members with full privileges, including voting. The membership of the committee ranges in size from 20 to 200, depending on county population and voting patterns.

What is a state central committee? The state central committee conducts campaigning and fundraising on the state level. State party chairs serve four-year terms and cannot succeed themselves. The chair alternates between northern and southern California. Party membership is very large. For the Republican, Democratic, and American Independent parties, the state central committee includes all party officeholders and nominees at the state level as well as numerous appointees of elected officials and of the county central committees. The Democratic committee is the largest (over 2,800 members), because it includes an additional 400 local representatives chosen at Assembly district caucuses throughout the state. The state central committees of the Libertarian and Peace & Freedom parties are composed of the members of the county central committee.

What are unofficial party organizations? Some of the continuous work of the party is done by voluntary political groups which are not a part of the organization and are not bound by the laws governing parties. These groups provide

June 2012 primary voters by political party:

Democrat: 43.66 percent
Republican: 29.36 percent
American Independent: 2.66 percent
Green Party: .60 percent
Peace and Freedom: .34 percent
Americans Elect: .02 percent

No party preference: 20.94 percent

a forum for party members of similar convictions, and work to influence their party's policies by supporting candidates who represent their views. Unlike the official parties, they are free to endorse candidates in the primary election, a crucial time for influencing the direction of party policy. Unofficial party organizations that have had a significant influence on politics in California include the California Democratic Council, the Federation of Young Democrats, the California Republican Assembly, the United Republicans of California, and the California Republican League.

CHAPTER 3

How Ballot Measures Get on the Ballot

<www.sos.ca.gov/elections/ballot-measures>

Citizens of California expect their elected representatives in the Senate and Assembly to pass laws and keep government running. If they are dissatisfied with what the legislators are doing, California voters can also directly propose new laws or repeal ones that have been passed. They do this by using the powers of initiative and referendum, which have been in place since 1911.

What does that mean?

Initiative: a law proposed by a group of citizens by means of a petition containing the signatures of the required number of voters. Initiatives can propose a new law (statutory initiative) or amend the state constitution.

Referendum: a vote on whether a law passed by the legislature and signed by the governor should be enacted.

IF YOU WANT TO PROPOSE AN INITIATIVE:

< http://www.
sos.ca.gov/
elections/
ballot-
measures/
how-qualify-
initiative/>

1. Draft the text of the proposed law or constitutional amendment. If you form a group of 25 or more qualified voters, you can get help in drafting the initiative from the lawyers who work for the Legislature. You can also ask the Secretary of State to review the draft for clarity.

2. Submit the draft, along with $200 to the Attorney General. If the measure qualifies for the ballot within two years of the summary date, the money is refunded.

3. The Attorney General posts the initiative on a public Web site for 30 days. During this time, the public may comment on the proposed initiative and you may make revisions. At the end of the 30 days, the Attorney General's office prepares the title and summary.

For information and help with intitiatives, contact the Secretary of State's initiative coordinator: 916.657.2166.

4. Complete the petition process within the deadline set by the Secretary of State. Deadlines are calculated after the Secretary of State receives a copy of the title and summary from the Attorney General. Proponents have 180 days, or about six months, in which to gather signatures and file the petition.

5. Circulate the draft of your petition for signatures. Only people currently eligible to be voters are entitled to circulate and only registered voters may sign a petition. Each qualified voter may sign an initiative petition only once.

6. When you have collected 25 percent of the required signatures, submit a formal statement verifying this to the Secretary of State. The Secretary of State then sends copies of the initiative to the Legislature for hearings on the proposed measure. Though the Legislature has no authority to alter the measure or prevent it from going to the ballot, these hearings give an opportunity for the Legislature and proponents to determine if there is a possibility of enacting legislation instead of putting the initiative on the ballot.

November 2010: 10,095,185 votes cast for governor

7. When all the signatures are gathered, file the signed petitions with the election officials in the counties in which the signatures were gathered. All petitions circulated in one county must be filed at the same time. Election officials check the total number of valid signatures by verifying a random sample of them.

8. Find out whether your petition qualifies for the ballot. The number of signatures required to qualify a measure for the ballot is based on the number of people who voted for any candidate for governor in the last election. An initiative to change the Constitution requires at least eight percent of the number of votes for governor. A statutory initiative—an initiative to enact or change a law—requires at least five percent of the votes for governor.

9. Organize the campaign for the initiative. Arguments for and against the initiative are printed in the ballot pamphlet that is mailed to all voter households.

10. File a financial disclosure statement. There are no restrictions on amount of money contributed or spent to support or oppose initiative measures. The Fair Political Practices Commission regularly reports the campaign financial information to the public.

11. Vote on the measures. An initiative passes if it is approved by a majority of those voting on the measure. Once it is adopted, the law can only be changed by voters in another election, unless the initiative statute itself contains a specific provision allowing the legislature to amend it.

LIMITATIONS ON THE USE OF INITIATIVES:

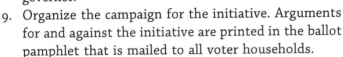

- Initiatives are limited to one subject. The California Supreme Court has held that a measure meets the single subject test if all of its parts are *"reasonably germane."*

Only 24 states allow voters to place initiatives on the ballot.

- An initiative may not name a person to office.
- An initiative may not be used to assign a duty or power to a particular private corporation.

All 50 states allow legislators to put issues on the ballot.

LEGISLATURE'S USE OF INITIATIVE

Most ballot measures are placed on the ballot by the legislature rather than by citizen petitions. The California State Legislature

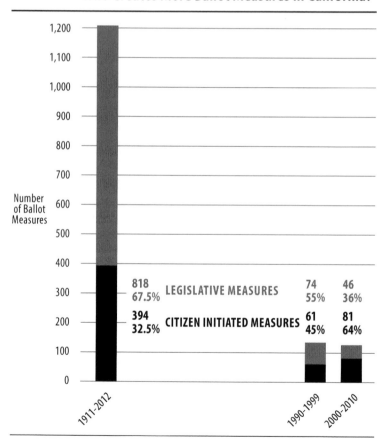

Figure 3.1   **Who Creates More Ballot Measures in California?**

frequently uses its authority to put measures on the ballot in the form of legislative referenda, bond measures and constitutional amendments.[1]

See Figure 3.1.

[1] League of Women Voters® California: *Initiative and Referendum in California: A Legacy Lost? Study Guide. p. 20. <ca.lwv.org/sites/lwvc.org/files/ downloads/studies/study-guide-12-07-2012.pdf>.*

Background and History of Initiatives in California

After initiatives were introduced in 1912, they were used by a wide variety of interest groups for many different purposes. Topics covered give us insight into what voters were concerned with over the years. A sample of measures passed during different time periods include:

1912–1932
- Abolition of the poll tax
- Regulation of prize fights
- Chiropractic licensing
- Osteopathic licensing
- Klamath River Fish and Game District
- Legislative reapportionment
- Voter registration
- State liquor regulation

1933–1952
- Selection of judges
- State civil service
- Fishing control
- Funds for elementary schools
- Aged and Blind Act
- Daylight Saving Time
- Public housing projects

1953–1982
- Student school assignment
- Political reform act
- Property tax limitation (Prop 13)
- Gift and inheritance taxes
- Limitation of government appropriations
- Income tax indexing
- Criminal justice
- Nuclear weapons

1984–2010
- State lottery
- Insurance rates
- Public employees retirement
- Campaign contributions
- Tribal casinos
- Definition of marriage
- Water quality
- Redistricting of congressional districts

Between 1912 and January 2015, according to the Secretary of State, a total of 1,828 initiatives were circulated. Of these, 1,367 failed to qualify for the ballot. A total of 363 initiatives qualified for the ballot and 123 of these were approved by the voters.

PROPOSALS FOR CHANGE

The ideal that every citizen in a nation has the right to be heard is the dream of democratic government. Direct democracy, and specifically the initiative and referendum process, enables and encourages citizen participation in government and is used in many states in various forms.

Direct democracy began in Athens, Greece, about 2500 years ago.

Issues with Relying on Ballot Measures to Solve Public Problems:

- Making law by ballots pits one side against another
- Rigidity; difficult to correct errors
- Influence of money
- Judicial review increasingly needed due to by-passing legislative checks and balances
- Conflicting ballot measures; confusion of campaigns
- Less accountability from representatives
- More potential to harm minority interests

The California model worked fairly well, with relatively little use, from the time of its adoption in 1911 until the passage of Proposition 13 in 1978. As an indicator of a deeper dissatisfaction with government generally, Prop 13's success showed an initiative to be an available, practicable alternative to passing laws and constitutional amendments when the elected legislature failed to do so. The use of initiative, however, has limited the flexibility of state government to find consensus and respond to emerging issues. Prop 13 also redirected the way public funds were allocated, leaving the state far more powerful than counties and towns. The initiative not only limited the amount of property tax that any level of government could charge, but directed that all the income from property tax would flow through Sacramento before being distributed to the cities, counties, and school districts in the state.

 Perhaps the greatest impact, of late, of the increasing use of the initiative has been to direct portions of the state budget to specific issues or activities chosen by voters. Unfortunately, as time passes, more and more of the budget is allocated by voter mandate. Even initiatives that do not directly affect the budget may in fact do so as an unintended consequence—for example, the Third Strike law has increased the prison population and thus the required funding. All of this combined with the fact that raising any new revenues requires a two-thirds vote of the Legislature leaves an elected leadership that has less control of the budget and in turn is viewed as increasingly ineffective.

Regardless of the consequences of its growing impact, the initiative and referendum are today the most popular elements in California's governmental structure. Voters find the process satisfying because it means they have a choice, they have their voices heard, and the issue is settled by an election unless it is challenged in the courts.

While some observers fear the growing inflexibility of state government, the generally preferred solution is to mend, not end, direct democracy. The continued value of these policy-making tools calls out for reforms to re-introduce a more sensitive and fairer process of making law. These reforms are intended to reduce the need to spend large amounts of money to get an initiative on the ballot and to give all citizens an equal opportunity to place measures on the ballot.

Most proposals to change the initiative process center on five issues:
- the necessity for court action
- the role of money
- a lack of substantive information for voters
- the role of legislators

Some experts suggest that drafting could be improved if each initiative measure had to be reviewed by an official authority for clarity. Some seek further definition of the single subject rule. Others propose to change the number of signatures necessary to qualify; require a certain geographic distribution of signatures; change the time allowed to collect signatures; or forbid paying those who solicit signatures.

Various limitations have been suggested for the campaign stage. These include limiting the amount an individual or group can contribute; requiring more complete disclosure of contributors; providing public financing for initiative campaigns; providing more public hearings and writing simpler analyses in the voter pamphlet.

Prior to 1966, proponents could pursue either the direct or the indirect initiative route. Under the indirect form, the proposal was submitted first to the legislature. The Legislature had 40 days to enact or reject the proposal. If the Legislature adopted it without change, it became law. If the Legislature rejected it or failed to act, the initiative went on to the ballot for decision by the people. This indirect procedure was used so infrequently that it was repealed in 1966. Yet interest in this form of the initiative continues to be expressed. Nearly every legislative session since 1985 has included attempts to reinstate the indirect initiative process.

In 2014, the legislature enacted a measure (SB 1253) which:

- Increased the number of days for circulating an initiative petition from 150 to 180 days
- Changed the timing of legislative hearings to be earlier in the process – after 25 percent of the required signatures have been gathered rather than after a measure has fully qualified
- Allowed proponents to withdraw a measure that has already qualified for the ballot up to 130 days before an election on that measure.

These changes create an opportunity for proponents of a measure and the Legislature to work together on a legislative alternative to an initiative.

REFERENDUMS

 California is one of 24 states that use the petition form of referendum. Using petition reform, voters can demand that a measure enacted by the Legislature and signed by the governor be referred to the electorate before going into effect. Unlike an initiative, which proposes a new law, a referendum requests the reconsideration of a law that has already been passed by the legislature and signed by the governor. A referendum asks whether the law be enacted as it was passed or not.

The state Constitution defines an urgency statute as one *"necessary for the immediate preservation of the public peace, health, or safety."* An urgency statute passes the Legislature only if it is approved by a two-thirds vote in each house; it cannot be referred to the voters through the referendum process.

 ### If You Want to Bring a Referendum to the Voters:

1. **Titling**. Before circulating a referendum petition, submit it to the Attorney General for a title and summary.

2. **Circulating**. Allow 90 days to complete the entire process of circulating petitions and verifying that the required number of valid signatures has been submitted. This three-month period begins the day a bill is enacted.

In 2012, the total number of required signatures was 504,760

3. **Qualifying**. A petition referendum qualifies for the ballot if it is signed by voters equal in number to 5 percent of those who cast votes in the governor's race in the most recent gubernatorial election. The total number of signatures required as of 2015 is 365,880.

4. **Voting**. The law or section of the law that is challenged takes effect only if it is approved by a majority of those voting on the question in the next election. The governor is permitted to call a special election for consideration of a referendum. The Legislature is permitted to amend or repeal referendum statutes.

Use of Referendums

Referendums have not been used as often as initiatives. Between 1912 and 2011, 75 referendums were circulated and either qualified for the ballot or were rejected. Fewer subjects have been addressed by referendum than by initiative. Measures dealing with oil production, drilling on tidelands owned by the state, and taxation on oleomargarine were among the early topics.

Legislative decisions were challenged and referred to the voters with the greatest frequency during the 1920s and 1930s. In 1952, a measure dealing with tax exemptions of nonprofit schools was approved in a referendum vote in a close decision. The referendum then fell into a period of disuse for almost 30 years. In June 1982, two issues reached the ballot by the referendum process. That year the Legislature had passed measures addressing district reapportionment and construction of state water facilities. The voters rejected the Legislature's plan in both instances. After that no referendum appeared on the ballot until 2000, when voters rejected an Indian Gambling statute. In recent years most state referendums have dealt with Indian gaming Laws.

The U.S. Constitution makes no provision for national referendums. A constitutional amendment would be required to allow them.

LOCAL DIRECT LEGISLATION

Initiatives and referendums can be used by local governments as well as by the state. They have been used more often by city governments than by counties.

Charter cities establish their own procedures. General law cities and counties operate under provisions of the state elections code, which includes the initiative and referendum. In these cities, proponents submit a proposal to the city or county clerk, whichever is appropriate. They must publish a notice of intent to circulate an initiative petition.

 ## What does that mean?

Charter city: a city that is governed by its own legally adopted document (charter). Charter cities may have a city manager or a city council or other system of government.

General law city: a city that has not adopted a charter, so is governed by state law. These cities are governed by a five-person city council.

Petition circulators at the local level have 180 days to qualify a local initiative or referendum, as opposed to 180 days to qualify a statewide initiative and 90 days to qualify a statewide referendum.

At the municipal level the total signatures required is based on a percentage of the city's registered voters. The signature requirements at the county level are based on the number of votes cast within that county for candidates for governor in the last election.

In cities of 1000+, a special election petition requires signatures from at least 15 percent of voters.

A completed initiative petition is presented to the appropriate elected body, either the city council or the board of supervisors. The elected body may adopt the proposal without change, thereby ending the process. If the council or board refuses to act or wishes to make changes, the proposition is submitted to the voters at the next regular election. In cities of 1,000 people or more, if the petitions are signed by 15 percent or more of the voters, the council or board must call a special election to decide the issue.

Separating the Powers

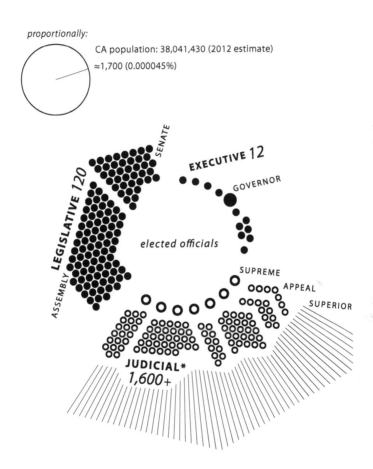

proportionally:

CA population: 38,041,430 (2012 estimate)

≈1,700 (0.000045%)

SENATE

EXECUTIVE 12

GOVERNOR

LEGISLATIVE 120

elected officials

ASSEMBLY

SUPREME

APPEAL

SUPERIOR

JUDICIAL*
1,600+

*California Supreme, Appellate, and Superior Court judges are usually appointed by the Governor and subject to voter approval in the following election.

Legislative Branch

California's state government is divided into three main branches: the legislative branch makes laws; the executive branch administers and enforces laws; and the judicial branch interprets laws and passes judgment on whether specific actions are legal or illegal. Chapters 4, 5, and 6 examine each of these branches in turn.

There are some exceptions to the normally distinct roles of each branch because of the system of checks and balances set up in the Constitution. For example, the governor, as chief executive of the state, has the authority to veto legislation and legislators are constitutionally authorized to serve on certain administrative boards in the executive branch.

For information about current or past legislation, see <leginfo. legislature. ca.gov/>.

LEGISLATIVE POWERS

Every year the Legislature adopts hundreds of new laws or makes changes in existing laws, in response to new situations and needs.

The subject matter of state laws is limited by certain federal restrictions. When state and federal laws conflict, federal laws usually prevail, although California can impose stricter standards than comparable federal legislation on some issues such as environmental protection and firearms possession. The U.S. Supreme Court has extended federal jurisdiction into the areas of civil and criminal rights, primarily on the basis of the Bill of Rights and the Fourteenth Amendment, which declares:

No state shall make or enforce any law which shall abridge the privileges or immunities of citizens of the United States; nor shall any state deprive any person of life, liberty, or property without due process of law; nor deny to any person within its jurisdiction the equal protection of the laws.

The Legislature has broad power over local governments. Counties, cities, regional agencies, and special districts may be created only in accordance with state law. When local ordinances and state laws conflict or cover the same subject, state laws generally prevail.

The Legislature controls public finances by levying taxes and appropriating funds. (See chapter 10).

As part of the system of checks and balances, the Legislature has control over some aspects of the administrative agencies of the executive branch.

Questions about an agency? Contact your representative's local office.

The Legislature can regulate the

- funding of agencies
- organization of agencies
- procedures of agencies.

It can also

- appoint citizens to policymaking committees in the executive branch
- designate members of the Legislature to serve on agency boards
- approve many appointments made by the governor.

The Legislature's role in the impeachment process serves as a check on both the executive and judicial branches. The state Assembly has the power to impeach—that is, to accuse an elected state official or judge of misconduct in office; the Senate tries impeachment cases.

THE LEGISLATORS

The California Legislature has two branches:

State Assembly

- 1 representative elected in each of 80 districts
- Districts are numbered consecutively from north to south
- Each district represents approximately 465,000 residents

State Senate

- 1 representative elected in each of 40 districts
- Districts are numbered consecutively from north to south
- Each district represents approximately 930,000 residents

Find your representative (Senate or Assembly) at <findyourrep.legislature.ca.gov/>.

Redistricting

Every ten years, following the federal census, the political district boundaries from which our representatives are elected must be adjusted to make the districts equal in population. This process is known as "redistricting." See <sos.ca.gov/elections/ca-redistricting.htm>.

Consequently, a district in a rural, sparsely populated area is much larger, geographically, than one in an urban, densely populated area. The lines of the districts are adjusted after each national census to reflect changes in the population. The census is taken at the beginning of each decade and the district boundary lines are adjusted in the following year.

For many years the Legislature determined the boundaries for the congressional, state Senate, state Assembly, and Board of Equalization districts in the state after the completion of each national census. However, the passage of California Proposition 11, the *Voters First Act*, by voters in November 2008, changed that system. This Act authorized the establishment of a *California Citizens Redistricting Commission*, a 14-member commission consisting of five Democrats, five Republicans, and four commissioners from neither major party. The commissioners were selected in November and December 2010 and were required to complete the new maps by August 15, 2011.

Following the 2010 passage of California Proposition 20, the *Voters First Act for Congress*, the commission was also assigned the responsibility of redrawing the state's U.S. congressional district boundaries. The primary criteria for redistricting is creating districts of roughly equal population and respecting the requirements of the federal Voting Rights Act. District boundaries must also meet certain criteria under state law including:

- maintaining contiguous geographical borders
- keeping cities, counties, neighborhoods, and communities of interest whole
- disregarding consideration of political parties, incumbents, or candidates.

The Commission must solicit public comment on the proposed redistricting plans it develops. The redistricting plans may also be subject to voter approval under the state's referendum process or be challenged before the state Supreme Court or federal courts, depending on the office in question.

What does that mean?

A "community of interest" is defined in the California Constitution as "a contiguous population which shares common social and economic interests that should be included within a single district for purposes of its effective and fair representation."

Californians are eligible to apply for a seat on the Commission if:

- They have been continuously registered in California with the same political party, or with no political party, for the five years immediately prior to being appointed to the Commission
- They have voted in at least two of the last three statewide general elections.
- They have no conflicts of interest as outlined in the Voters First Act.

For more information about applications: <wedrawthelines. ca.gov/downloads/voters_first_act.pdf>.

ELIGIBILITY AND ELECTION

Requirements

Each legislator must

- be a U.S. citizen 18 years of age or older
- be a registered voter and otherwise qualified to vote for that office at the time nomination papers are issued to the person

Term Limits

- A person who was first elected to the Assembly or Senate on or after passage of Proposition 28 on June 5, 2012, may serve no more than a combined total of twelve years in the Senate, the Assembly, or both.
- A person elected to the Assembly before passage of Proposition 28 may serve a maximum of three two-year terms. A person elected to the state Senate before passage of Proposition 28 is limited to two four-year terms in the Senate and three two-year terms in the Assembly.

Prop 140 established term limits in 1990. Since then at least 30 new members have been elected every two years.

Prop 28, passed by the voters in June 2012, reduced the maximum number of years an elected official could serve in the Legislature from 14 to 12.

Elections

- All 80 Assembly seats are up for election for a two-year term every even-numbered year.
- Half of the 40 Senate seats are up for election for a four-year term every even-numbered year.
- A vacancy is filled by a special election announced by the governor.

LEGISLATIVE ETHICS

The official conduct of members of the Legislature and legislative staff are regulated by the California Constitution and the Political Reform Act. These regulations include:

- limits on gifts from lobbyists and others
- a ban on speaking fees
- rules governing conflicts of interest
- a requirement to disclose personal financial interests.

Per Diem: An allowance for daily expenses

The law also provides that legislative resources may be used only for legislative purposes, not for personal or campaign purposes. Members of the Legislature, most legislative staff, and registered lobbyists must attend an ethics orientation course once in every two-year session. Each house of the Legislature has an ethics committee responsible for training, advice, and investigation of complaints, and has the power to judge the qualifications and election of its members.

COMPENSATION

Compensation is set annually by the California Citizens Compensation Commission (CCCC). <calhr. ca.gov/cccc/Pages/ home.aspx>.

As of 2012, members of the California Legislature are paid $95,290.56 per year. They are also given per diem (daily allowance) of $141.86 per day in session. Members elected after 1990 do not receive a pension from the state. This compensation is higher than the compensation of legislators in the other 49 states.

Figure 4.1 **Senate and Assembly Leadership**

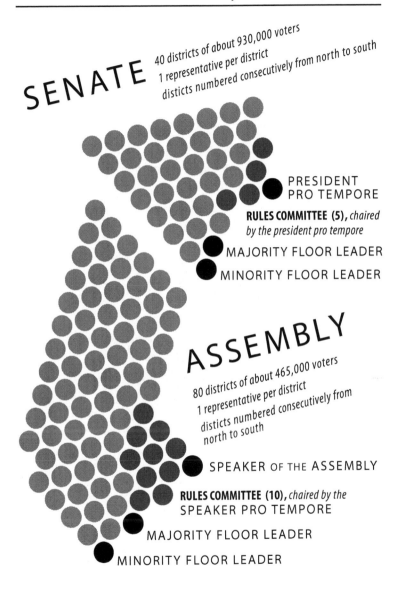

SENATE
40 districts of about 930,000 voters
1 representative per district
disticts numbered consecutively from north to south

● PRESIDENT
PRO TEMPORE

RULES COMMITTEE (5), *chaired by the president pro tempore*

● MAJORITY FLOOR LEADER
● MINORITY FLOOR LEADER

ASSEMBLY
80 districts of about 465,000 voters
1 representative per district
disticts numbered consecutively from north to south

● SPEAKER OF THE ASSEMBLY

RULES COMMITTEE (10), *chaired by the* SPEAKER PRO TEMPORE

● MAJORITY FLOOR LEADER
● MINORITY FLOOR LEADER

2012 *population figures, subject to change with each census and interim adjustments for redistricting*

SENATE LEADERSHIP

State Senate
Motto:
SENATORIS
EST CIVITAS
LIBERTATEM
TUERI

It is the duty
of a senator
to guard the
liberty of the
common-
wealth

The **lieutenant governor** is the ex officio president of the Senate, but has no official role in routine business and votes only in the case of a tie vote.

The **President pro tempore**, elected by the members of the Senate, is responsible for the overall administration of the Senate, chairs the Senate Rules Committee, promotes the prompt disposition of bills, and organizes other business before the Senate. He or she is also political leader of the majority party.

The **Senate Rules Committee**, chaired by the president pro tempore, is composed of four other members elected by the state Senate. This committee has the power to

- appoint all other Senate committees
- designate chairs and vice chairs of standing committees
- decide which committee will consider each bill
- make recommendations on the confirmation of many gubernatorial appointments
- decide which senators will serve on executive and judicial boards and commissions
- approve all expenditures and claims for reimbursement by Senate committees.

The **majority and minority floor leaders** are chosen by their respective party caucuses to manage political strategy. The majority and minority party caucuses also elect their own chairs to lead party policy meetings.

ASSEMBLY LEADERSHIP

State Assembly
Motto:
LEGISLATORUM
EST JUSTAS
LEGES CONDERE

The **speaker of the Assembly**, the presiding officer of that body, is elected from and by the Assembly membership and serves ex officio on all Assembly and joint legislative committees. The speaker has a number of powers, including the following:

- names the majority floor leader and the chair of the rules committee
- assists in establishing the size and membership of all standing committees
- designates the chairs and vice chairs of policy committees, who must be from opposite political parties
- selects members for executive and judicial boards and commissions.

The **speaker pro tempore** is elected by the Assembly to perform leadership duties during the speaker's absence. The speaker pro tem is an ex officio member of the rules committee with no vote.

The **Assembly Rules Committee** is chaired by the speaker or the speaker's appointee. The majority and minority caucuses each nominate four additional members; the eight nominees must be approved by majority vote of the Assembly. The rules committee refers bills to committees and selects and supervises Assembly support staff. It is responsible for expediting procedures and proposing changes in Assembly rules. Members of this committee may not chair standing committees.

The **floor leader of the majority party** is elected by the majority party caucus; the **minority floor leader** is chosen by the minority caucus.

The **majority and minority caucus chairs** are chosen by their respective parties.

LEGISLATIVE COMMITTEES

Policy committees are standing committees established in the rules adopted by each house; their membership usually changes after each election. Some establish subcommittees to facilitate their work. Each committee is assigned bills in its subject area to hear, study, and vote on. Committee names change slightly from session to session, but each house (Assembly and Senate) has committees which deal with similar issue areas including:

It is the duty of the legislators to pass just laws

Ex officio: serving because of your job, office, or position.

Caucus: a group within a political party that meets to decide policy or select candidates. A caucus can be based on regional, political, ethnic, or other factors. Their meetings are also called caucuses.

- agriculture and water resources
- banking, commerce, and international trade
- business and professions
- consumer protection
- constitutional amendments
- education
- energy
- environmental safety
- government organization
- health and human services
- housing
- insurance
- industrial relations and labor
- local government
- public employees and retirement
- revenue and taxation
- other topics as needed

In the interim period between legislative sessions, committees can meet to gather information and make recommendations, though they may not take official actions. Interim hearings are sometimes held outside Sacramento to permit testimony by experts and residents in different parts of the state.

Fiscal committees are standing committees that handle the annual state budget and all other bills with either a direct or implied cost to the state. Bills with fiscal implications, often the most important bills, are referred to fiscal committees from policy committees.

Special or select committees may be set up by either house to research a comparatively limited subject, such as child abuse or climate change.

Joint committees include members of both houses, appointed by the speaker in the Assembly and by the rules committee in the Senate. Such committees can conduct investigations, hold hearings, and recommend legislation.

Conference committees, set up to resolve differences in the Assembly and Senate versions of bills, are composed of three members of each house, chosen by the Assembly speaker and the Senate Rules Committee.

LEGISLATIVE STAFF

Each member of the Legislature is entitled to an administrative assistant and secretaries for both district and capitol offices. Additional personnel are provided for larger districts or workloads. Most employees of the Legislature are appointed by the rules committee in each house and are exempt from civil service regulations.

Each committee chair is provided one or more committee consultants, depending on the workload of the particular committee. Especially knowledgeable in their subject areas, committee consultants analyze bills, help draft legislation, plan hearings, and conduct studies.

Offices of research provide services for each house. The majority and minority party caucuses in each house are assisted by consultants.

Legislative and committee staff are usually policy experts in specific areas. When you contact them, they can communicate your concerns to the legislator.

LEGISLATIVE PROCEDURES

The state Constitution defines specific dates on which, and number of days in which, the Legislature must complete certain procedures. Within this framework, each house determines its own standing rules of procedure.

Each session is convened under the standing rules of the previous session. Each house then adopts the same or new rules to govern procedural matters—such as the committee system, duties of officers, order of daily business, parliamentary rules, and joint legislative rules—for the new session.

LEGISLATIVE SESSIONS

The governor is constitutionally authorized to call the Legislature into special session at any time to deal with urgent or extraordinary issues. Action during a special session is limited to the subjects specified by the governor. Procedural rules permit speedier action during a special session than a regular session. Laws passed in special session take effect 91 days after the session adjourns.

The new Legislature convenes each two-year session for an organizational meeting in December after each general election, and then recesses until early January. A regular session lasts two years. The meeting schedule is as follows:

Figure 4.2 The Legislature: Meeting Schedule

	ODD-NUMBERED YEARS
JANUARY	regular session resumes
SPRING	one-week recess
SUMMER	one-month recess
SEPTEMBER-DECEMBER	interim study recess

	EVEN-NUMBERED YEARS
JANUARY	regular session resumes
SPRING	one-week recess
SUMMER	one-month recess
AUGUST 31ST	end of regular session
NOVEMBER 30TH	adjournment
DECEMBER	new legislative session begins

TYPES OF LEGISLATION

Legislative actions are taken in the form of bills (proposed laws) and resolutions of various types:

- An Assembly bill (AB) is one introduced in the Assembly—numbered in the order presented for each legislative session.

- A Senate bill (SB) is introduced in the Senate, also numbered in order presented.

- Resolutions are the means by which the Legislature takes an action that does not require a bill.

- A constitutional amendment—known as an ACA or SCA, depending on the house of origin—is a resolution proposing a change in the Constitution. An ACA or SCA must be approved by two-thirds of the members of each house by a certain deadline in order to qualify for a statewide ballot. A constitutional amendment must be approved by a majority of voters to take effect.

- A concurrent resolution is used to adopt joint rules, establish joint committees, commend persons or organizations, or express legislative intent. Referred to as an ACR or SCR, depending on the house of origin, a concurrent resolution needs only a majority vote of each house to pass and does not need the governor's signature.

- A joint resolution, referred to as an AJR or SJR, depending on the house of origin, usually urges passage or defeat of legislation pending before the U.S. Congress or urges presidential action.

- A house resolution expresses the sentiment of either the Assembly (AR) or Senate (SR). A house resolution is used, for example, to create an interim committee, amend a house rule, or congratulate an individual or group; it is usually adopted by majority voice vote.

LEGISLATIVE PROCESS

The Legislature handles bills according to a process prescribed by the Constitution and statutory law *to ensure opportunity for citizen input*. See <leginfo.ca.gov/bil2lawx.html>.

The legislative process, outlined above, is divided into 11 stages.

1. **Drafting**. Upon the request of a legislator, the Legislative Counsel's Office drafts the formal language of a bill and a summary (called a digest) of its main provisions. Ideas for proposals often come from individuals, legislative committees, the executive branch, counties, cities, businesses, lobbyists, and citizen groups.

2. **Introduction**. A bill can be introduced in the Assembly or in the Senate. There it is numbered and read for the first time. (The Constitution requires, with limited exception, that a bill be read by title on three separate days in each house.) The name of the author (the legislator who introduced the bill) becomes part of the title. A bill cannot be heard or acted upon until after a 30-day waiting period.

3. **Policy committee**. The rules committee of the house of origin assigns each bill to a policy committee appropriate to the subject matter. The committee hears public testimony from the author, proponents, and opponents. The committee can pass the original or an amended form of the bill, kill it by holding it in committee, refer it to another committee, amend it and re-refer it to itself, send it to interim study, or take no action. Approval of a bill requires a majority of those on the committee.

4. **Fiscal committee**. If approved by the policy committee, a bill which contains an appropriation or has financial implications for the state is sent to the fiscal committee, where similar consideration and actions can occur. Approval of a bill requires a majority of those on the committee.

Figure 4.3   ## Typical Path of Legislation

suggestions for legislation *from a variety of sources*

LEGISLATIVE COUNSEL   legislation drafted at legislator's request

SENATE *or* ASSEMBLY

	bill introduced, first reading
RULES COMMITTEE	assigned to committee
POLICY COMMITTEE	public testimony

PASS / FAIL

FISCAL COMMITTEE   public testimony

PASS / FAIL

HOUSE FLOOR	second reading
FLOOR debate and vote	third reading

PASS / FAIL

repeat process in the other house

POLICY COMMITTEE	public testimony	P / F
FISCAL COMMITTEE	public testimony	P / F
FLOOR debate and vote	third reading	P / F

possible results:	passed second house without change
	concurrence, with amendments
	CONFERENCE COMMITTEE *to resolve differences*

to GOVERNOR

possible results:	signed into law
	becomes law without signature

VETOED *override possible by* LEGISLATURE

effective date

5. **Second reading**. A bill recommended for passage by committee is read a second time on the floor of the house. Ordinarily there is little or no debate. If a bill is amended at this stage, it may be referred back for another committee hearing.

6. **Floor vote**. A bill is read a third time, debated, and possibly amended on the floor. A roll call vote is taken. An ordinary bill needs a majority vote to pass (21 votes in the Senate, 41 votes in the Assembly). An urgency bill or a bill with fiscal implications requires a two-thirds vote (27 votes in the Senate, 54 in the Assembly).

7. **Second house**. If it receives a favorable vote in the first house, a bill repeats the same steps in the other house. If the second house passes the bill without changing it, it is sent to the governor's desk.

8. **Concurrence or conference**. If a measure is amended in the second house and passed, it is returned to the house of origin for consideration of amendments. The house of origin may concur with the amendments and send the bill to the governor, or reject the amendments and submit it to a two-house conference committee. If either house rejects the conference report, a second (and even a third) conference committee can be formed. If both houses adopt the conference report, the bill is sent to the governor.

9. **Governor's action**. Within 12 days after receiving a bill, the governor may sign it into law, allow it to become law without a signature, or veto it. In bills that appropriate funds, the governor may veto or reduce particular expenditure items while approving the rest of the provisions. When the Legislature recesses in mid-September of an odd-numbered year, the governor has until mid-October to make decisions on bills. When the Legislature concludes its work in August of an even-numbered year, the governor has until September 30 to make decisions on bills.

10. **Overrides**. A vetoed bill is returned to the house of origin, where a vote may be taken to override the governor's veto; a two-thirds vote of both houses is required to override a veto.

11. **Effective date**. Ordinarily a law passed during a regular session takes effect January 1 of the following year. A few statutes go into effect as soon as the governor signs them; these include acts calling for elections and urgency measures necessary for the immediate preservation of the public peace, health, or safety.

TRACKING LEGISLATION

Bills that are going through the Legislature are listed on the California State Legislature Website <leginfo.ca.gov/>. The Bill Information page with its daily updates makes it possible to search for the history and current status of each bill introduced in the current session, by number, sponsor or topic.

Information about bills introduced before 1993 is not available online, but information about them can be obtained by contacting the State Law Library at 916.654.0185.

PUBLIC INPUT

All Californians have the right to express their views on proposed measures, as individuals, in cooperation with others, and through legislative advocates. You can listen to live hearings, floor sessions and press conferences over the Internet. Senate proceedings are broadcast live on the California Channel, and can be viewed via cable television cable stations in communities all over California.

Public support or opposition to a bill or budget item can be expressed in many ways:

- E-mail messages to your state Senate or Assembly member.
- Telephone legislative offices in Sacramento or locally.
- Send letters to legislative representatives.
- Testify before committees.
- Visit legislative officials.
- Express your views on social media sites.
- Organize and participate in public information campaigns.

The easiest way to contact your senator or Assembly member is to visit the member's Web site and use the forms available there or follow directions for telephone calls or visits. Contact information is readily available at the California State Legislature Web site, <legisla­ture.ca.gov/legislators_and_districts/legislators/your_legislator.html>. If you do not have easy access to the Internet, you can go online at your local public library, or you can telephone the local office of your member of the state Senate or Assembly.

LOBBYISTS

Many organizations hire advocates or lobbyists to help present their views on legislative and administrative issues. Lobbyists must register with the Secretary of State each legislative session and file reports of their activities. The Secretary of State maintains the Cal-Access website <cal-access.ss.ca.gov/Lobbying/>, which lists information about lobbying activities, including the names of individual lobbyists and lobbying firms and links to copies of documents that are on file. See also information on the Fair Political Practices Commission website <fppc.ca.gov/index.php?id=4>.

Executive Branch Chapter 5

The governor holds the executive power of the state and is the sole official liaison between California state government, other state governments, and the federal government. The governor also takes part in the legislative process by proposing legislation and approving or disapproving legislation passed by both houses. After the California Senate and Assembly have written and approved the laws that will govern the state, these measures are sent to the executive branch and are subject to the governor's approval before becoming law. A governor may give approval to the bill with a signature, veto the bill (which can be overridden by a two-thirds majority vote of the Legislature), or do nothing and allow the bill to become law without any action by the governor.

There have been 39 governors, none of them women.

It is the duty of the executive branch to determine how to put laws into practice and then to enforce them. The governor is the official responsible for overseeing this process, with the help of eight elected executive officers and many appointed officials.

ROLE OF THE EXECUTIVE BRANCH

The legislative and executive branches often work together on initiating and shaping proposed legislation. Ideas for initiating or improving existing legislation often come from the executive branch as a result of its day-to-day operational experience in implementing laws and addressing new issues or problems. Although a final decision may be made by the department director, agency secretary, or the governor, staff members usually prepare information and position papers, and in many cases the higher official need only approve or disapprove.

José Antonio Ronaldo Pacheco (Feb.–Dec. 1875), was the 12th governor of California, the first born in the state, and the only Hispanic governor.

If legislation is required, procedures established by the governor's office are followed before the legislative counsel is requested to draft a bill or a legislator is asked to sponsor it. Any proposal which involves appropriation, federal funds, or future costs must be reviewed by the Department of Finance. The governor may also confer with legislators, department heads, agency secretaries, and others while the proposal is being formulated.

Legislators may request departments to help them prepare or review proposed legislation. Later, administrators may furnish further information or testify before legislative committees.

Many laws are broadly drawn, delegating to the executive units the power and responsibility of working out details as needed through administrative decisions and regulations. In practice, implementation of new laws often requires additional or more specific legislation.

EXECUTIVE OFFICIALS ELECTED BY VOTERS
(see Figure 5.1)

All elective officers in the executive branch

- serve four-year terms beginning the Monday after January 1 following their election

Figure 5.1 Elected Officers and the Cabinet

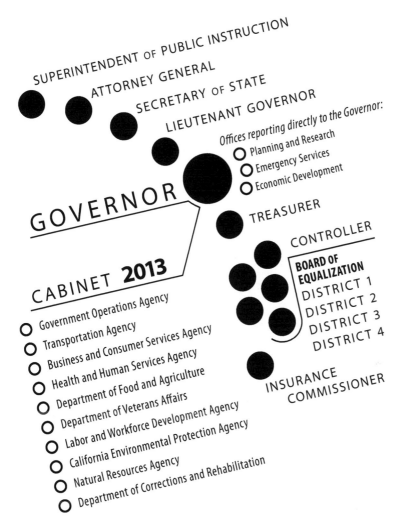

SUPERINTENDENT OF PUBLIC INSTRUCTION

ATTORNEY GENERAL

SECRETARY OF STATE

LIEUTENANT GOVERNOR

Offices reporting directly to the Governor:
- Planning and Research
- Emergency Services
- Economic Development

GOVERNOR

TREASURER

CONTROLLER

CABINET **2013**

- Government Operations Agency
- Transportation Agency
- Business and Consumer Services Agency
- Health and Human Services Agency
- Department of Food and Agriculture
- Department of Veterans Affairs
- Labor and Workforce Development Agency
- California Environmental Protection Agency
- Natural Resources Agency
- Department of Corrections and Rehabilitation

BOARD OF EQUALIZATION
DISTRICT 1
DISTRICT 2
DISTRICT 3
DISTRICT 4

INSURANCE COMMISSIONER

Agency/department secretaries are appointed by and report directly to the Governor. The role of the cabinet varies in different administrations and may play either a major or minor role in policy making. The secretaries direct and oversee the departments, bureaus, commissions and boards in each agency.

- are prohibited from serving more than two terms in the same office
- are subject to recall and impeachment

California Governor Earl Warren (1943–1953) became Chief Justice of the U.S. Supreme Court (1953–1969).

The governor fills vacancies by appointment unless the law provides otherwise. In the event of death, resignation, removal, or disability of the governor, the order of succession is: lieutenant governor, president pro tempore of the Senate, speaker of the Assembly, Secretary of State, attorney general, treasurer, and controller. If there is a question of the governor's disability, a commission established by law is authorized to petition the state Supreme Court to make a determination.

Governor <gov.ca.gov>

The California Constitution specifies that the governor must

- be a citizen of the United States and a resident of California
- * be registered and qualified to vote for the office at the time the nomination papers are issued to the person
- not have served two terms in that office since November 6, 1990

Governor Edmund G. "Jerry" Brown is the son of former Governor Edmund G. "Pat" Brown.

> *Article V, section 2 of the California Constitution requires five-year residency in California; however, it is the legal opinion of the Secretary of State's office that this provision violates the U.S. Constitution. (10/27/09)

Major powers of the office:
- broad powers of appointment over approximately 2000 positions, including all state department heads and officials and also several hundred members of boards and commissions; also fills unexpired terms of U.S. senators, supervisors in general law counties, and statewide officers when these positions have become vacant. When there are vacancies in the

offices of the superintendent of public instruction, the lieutenant governor, Secretary of State, controller, treasurer, attorney general, or on the state Board of Equalization, the governor nominates a person to fill the vacancy. This individual takes office upon confirmation by a majority of the membership of the Senate and of the Assembly.

- appointment of lawyers to fill judicial vacancies at the municipal and superior court level. For the Court of Appeals and California Supreme Court, gubernatorial nominees must be confirmed by the Commission on Judicial Appointments, and subsequently by the electorate at the first regular election thereafter.
- authority over organization and administration of the executive branch, other than elective officers and agencies administered by elective officers
- extensive financial controls
- commander in chief of the state militia, which can be called to active duty for civil disturbance or emergency, including natural disaster, or to enforce the law
- president of the Board of Regents of the University of California and the Board of Trustees of the California State University
- power to pardon, reprieve, and commute sentences, except in cases of impeachment
- performance of such duties as ribbon-cutting at public openings and appearing at parades and other celebrations as ceremonial head of state
- receives an annual salary of $165,288 (2013)

Governor Earl Warren (1943–1953) and Governor Jerry Brown (1975–1983; 2011–2015) are the only two people to be elected governor for more than two terms.

Salaries are set annually by the California Citizens Compensation Commission (cccc).

Lieutenant Governor

- assumes office of chief executive when governor is absent or unable to discharge duties
- presides over the Senate and may cast a tie-breaking vote on legislation

- represents the governor or performs other executive duties as requested
- chairs the Commission on Economic Development, which provides support and guidance to the governor, Legislature and private industry about the development of California's economy; serves ex officio on some boards and commissions
- receives an annual salary of 133,100 (2014)

Secretary of State

The SOS is the state election official

- serves as chief elections officer and records keeper for all federal and state elections; certifies the nomination and election of candidates; checks for the proper number of signatures for initiative, referendum, and recall petitions; prints the state ballot pamphlets; compiles reports of registration and official statements of the vote; implements electronic filing and Internet disclosure of campaign and lobbyist financial information; enforces election laws uniformly statewide
- provides introductory resources and services for anyone wanting to do business in California, connecting people with electronic versions of important documents and handbooks, searchable lists of registered businesses, and a step-by-step guide to starting a business
- oversees filings of articles of incorporation, limited partnerships, and related corporate documents; registration of trademarks; registration of deeds to state lands; filings of uniform commercial code division documents, such as liens against personal property, tax liens, and judgments; commissioning of notaries public
- operates the Safe at Home confidential address program; maintains the Domestic Partners and Advance Health Care Directive registries

- supervises the California State Archives
- receives an annual salary of 133,100 (2014)

State Controller

- serves as chief fiscal officer of the state
- keeps track of state money and pays state bills
- reports on the financial operations of state and local governments and informs the public of financial transactions of city, county and district governments
- collects some taxes and provides audit services to ensure that all taxes are collected
- manages the state's personnel payroll system including auditing and processing all personnel and payroll transactions for state civil service employees, exempt employees, and California State University employees
- chairs the California Public Employees' Retirement System (CalPERS), California State Teachers' Retirement System (CalSTRS), the Franchise Tax Board, and the California State Lands Commission
- serves as a member of more than 81 boards and commissions, including the Board of Equalization
- receives an annual salary of 141,973 (2014)

The state controller is the fifth member of the Board of Equalization.

State Treasurer

- acts as banker for the state, paying out state funds authorized by the controller
- serves as custodian of securities and other valuables deposited with the treasury
- sells state bonds and acts as investment officer for most state funds
- examines the financial soundness of major debt proposals of certain special districts
- serves on the boards of CalPERS and CalSTRS, which provide for the retirement of many state employees and also provide a variety of other services for them
- receives an annual salary of 141, 973 (2014)

Attorney General

Kamala Harris, elected in 2010, is the first woman to serve as Attorney General of California.

- serves as chief law enforcement officer of the state to see that laws are uniformly and adequately enforced
- interprets laws and renders opinions for the governor, state officers, the Legislature, and state agencies, boards and commissions
- manages the representation of the state and its officers in civil litigation and in appeals from superior courts in criminal cases
- establishes and operates projects and programs to protect Californians from fraudulent, unfair and illegal activities that victimize consumers or threaten public safety
- enforces laws that safeguard the environment and natural resources
- maintains central fingerprint and other databases
- administers the state's program of training for local law enforcement officers
- supervises all district attorneys and sheriffs and may act in the place of any district attorney if necessary
- prepares titles for all initiative and referendum petitions, and titles and digests for all state ballot measures
- receives an annual salary of 154,150 (2014)

Insurance Commissioner

- is responsible for protecting California's insurance consumers
- regulates the insurance industry and enforces the provisions of the California Insurance Code
- provides information to consumers on insurance rates, complaints about companies, and enforcement actions
- receives an annual salary of 141,973 (2014)

Board of Equalization

- consists of five members elected from four districts representing areas of the state, plus the state controller, serving concurrent four-year terms
- collects taxes and fees that provide approximately 34 percent of annual state revenue, including the state's sales and use, fuel, alcohol, tobacco, and other taxes, and collects fees that fund specific state programs. More than 1 million organizations are registered with the BOE
- ensures that county property tax assessment practices are equal and uniform throughout the state
- assesses the property of railroads and public utilities, including gas, electric, and telephone companies
- acts as appellate body for Franchise Tax Board decisions on taxes
- board members receive an annual salary of 133,100 (2014)

Superintendent of Public Instruction <cde.ca.gov/eo/>

- elected statewide on a nonpartisan basis for a four-year term
- directs the Department of Education (See Chapter 11)
- executes policies set by the State Board of Education appointed by the governor
- receives an annual salary of 154,150 (2014)

ORGANIZATION OF THE EXECUTIVE BRANCH

The operation of the governor's office varies with each governor, who decides how he or she wishes to manage liaisons with departments, the Legislature, and the public. These staff members are organized into units that assist with particular aspects of executive responsibility.

A major assistant to the governor is the chief of staff, who directs and supervises all units in the governor's office and serves as chief aide and as a member of the cabinet. Other important assistants include the administrative officer, press secretary, legislative secretary, appointments secretary (responsible for maintaining data on upcoming vacancies and potential appointees), and writing and research director.

Some offices report directly to the governor. As a part of a reorganization in 2012-13, the newly formed California Department of Human Resources, the Governor's Office of Emergency Services, the newly created Governor's Office of Business and Economic Development (GO-Biz), and the Governor's Office of Planning and Research report directly to the governor.

The Cabinet

As the governor's principal advisory and operational council, the cabinet gives the chief executive a comprehensive view of state operations and aids in policymaking and long-range planning. The governor appoints members and they serve at his or her pleasure. As of July 2013 there are ten cabinet secretaries heading the agencies of the state government. The role of the cabinet varies in different administrations and may play either a major or minor role in policymaking.

Agencies and Departments

Most departments in the state are grouped into agencies. The secretaries of the agencies provide leadership and policy guidance to their departments, serve as communication links between the governor and the departments, and review department budgets and legislative and administrative programs. The director of each department reports to the appropriate agency secretary, who coordinates related programs for resolution of problems that go beyond the authority of the department heads and is responsible for overall policy implementation. All communications to the cabinet go through the agency secretary, though frequently the secretary requests a department head to attend a cabinet meeting to present information or a position paper. The governor also sometimes holds briefing meetings with department heads. Some of the larger departments report directly to the governor.

The Government Operations Agency:
Departments that are involved in running the enterprise of state government, providing a single focus on state services, are part of CalGovOps:

- Department of General Services
- Department of Human Resources (CalHR)
- Department of Technology
- Office of Administrative Law
- Public Employees' Retirement System
- State Teachers' Retirement System
- State Personnel Board
- Victims Compensation and Government Claims Board
- Franchise Tax Board

Transportation Agency:
includes the following bodies:

- Department of Transportation (CALTRANS)
- Department of Motor Vehicles
- High-Speed Rail Authority
- California Highway Patrol
- California Transportation Commission
- Board of Pilot Commissioners
- Office of Traffic Safety
- New Motor Vehicle Board

Business, Consumer Services and Housing Agency:
Business and consumer-related departments that regulate or license industries, business activities, or professionals, including:

Questions or problems related to state agencies? Contact your state representative's district office. <findyourrep.legislature.ca.gov/>.

- Department of Consumer Affairs, which provides administrative and executive services for boards and commissions regulating licensed professionals, such as the State Board of Chiropractic Examiners, Bureau of Real Estate and Bureau of Real Estate Appraisers, and the Structural Pest Control Board
- Department of Housing and Community Development, which assists in the development and financing of affordable housing and administers general obligation bond programs
- Department of Fair Employment and Housing
- Department of Alcoholic Beverage Control
- California Horse Racing Board
- Seismic Safety Commission
- Department of Business Oversight, which provides the state's oversight of financial businesses
- Housing Financing Agency

Health and Human Services Agency:
- Department of Public Health
- Department of Health Care Services
- Department of Social Services
- Department of State Hospitals
- Department of Developmental Services
- Department of Managed Health Care
- Many other resources, including Covered California, Aging and Disability Resources, and the California Child Welfare Council

Department of Food and Agriculture

Department of Veterans Affairs

Labor and Workforce Development Agency:
- Unemployment Insurance Appeals Board

- Public Employment Relations Board
- Agricultural Labor Relations Board
- Employment Development Department
- Department of Industrial Relations
- Workforce Investment Board
- Employment Training Panel
- Department of Industrial Relations/
  Labor Commissioner

California Environmental Protection Agency:
- Department of Resources Recycling and Recovery
  (CalRecycle)
- Air Resources Board
- Department of Pesticide Regulation
- Department of Toxic Substances Control
- Office of Environmental Health Hazard Assessment
- State Water Resources Control Board

Natural Resources Agency:
- Seven departments are: Conservation, Conservation
  Corps, Fish and Wildlife, Forestry and Fire
  Protection, Parks and Recreation, Water Resources,
  Exposition Park
- Nine conservancies include Baldwin Hills,
  San Joaquin River, Santa Monica Mountains,
  and Sierra Nevada
- Seventeen boards and commissions include Coastal
  Commission, Central Valley Flood Protection Board,
  Boating and Waterways Commission, Wildlife
  Conservation Board, and Native American Heritage
  Commission
- Two museums: California Science Center and
  California African American Museum
- Three Councils: Biodiversity, Delta Stewardship,
  and Ocean Protection

Department of Corrections and Rehabilitation:
includes these divisions and boards:
- Adult Operations Division
- Adult Parole
- Juvenile Justice Division (includes Juvenile Parole Board)
- Correctional Health Care Services
- Board of Parole Hearings
- CCHCS Medical Contracts
- Council on Mentally Ill Offenders
- Facility Planning Construction and Management
- Prison Industry Authority
- Rehabilitation Programs

(Note: the Board of State and Community Corrections is now an independent agency providing oversight of California's adult and juvenile justice systems.)

The California Government Reorganization Process

In 1967 the Legislature recognized the governor's authority to reorganize the executive branch by approving the "executive reorganization" process. Under Government Code Section 12080.1, the governor from time to time shall examine the organization of all agencies and determine what changes are necessary to accomplish one or more of the following purposes:

- to promote the better execution of the laws and the expeditious administration of the public business
- to reduce expenditures and promote economy
- to increase the efficiency of the operation of state government to the fullest extent practicable
- to consolidate and coordinate agencies and functions according to major purposes
- to reduce the number of agencies by consolidating those having similar functions under a single head, for the efficient operation of the state government
- to eliminate overlapping and duplication of effort

The process for implementing reorganization is as follows:

1. The governor submits a reorganization plan to the Legislative Counsel for drafting into bill language, and to the Little Hoover Commission, which examines the plan and reports its recommendations to the Legislature.

2. Thirty days after submission to the Little Hoover Commission, the governor may submit the plan to the Legislature.

3. The plan becomes effective on the 61st calendar day of continuous session of the Legislature after the date on which the plan is submitted to the Legislature, or at a later date identified by the plan. The plan goes into effect unless either house passes a resolution disapproving the reorganization plan within the 60-day calendar period.

Legislation to formally approve and enact the reorganization is processed in the following year, but the reorganization is effective even without the statutes being on the books.

What does that mean?

The Little Hoover Commission is an independent, bipartisan board that studies and promotes efficiency, economy and improved service in state government. The commission is also charged with reviewing the governor's reorganization plans. <lhc.ca.gov/>.

Judicial Branch   Chapter 6

In addition to the executive and legislative branches of government, the judicial branch serves Californians. The judicial branch interprets state laws and oversees the administration of justice. These functions are carried out through a system of courts in California:

- California Supreme Court
- courts of appeal
- superior courts

The court system is independent of the executive and legislative branches, but they have a connection to the judicial branch. For example, the California Legislature passes the laws that the courts must enforce, and the governor influences the courts by appointing most judges. The role of the courts is to operate as a check on legislative and executive powers, making sure that these branches do not make or administer laws that are contrary to the California Constitution. The judiciary is responsible for ensuring that laws are justly and equitably applied in all matters brought before the courts.

RELATION OF STATE TO FEDERAL COURTS

The California court system exists side by side with the federal court system. The two systems converge in the United States Supreme Court, the final interpreter of the U.S. Constitution and of all federal law, which can be created by statute, treaty, administrative regulation, or the Constitution. The U.S. Supreme Court hears cases that were litigated in lower federal courts, or that involved federal constitutional law issues. The Supreme Court also determines whether state constitutions and laws conform to the U.S. Constitution. Also, state courts are bound by the Supreme Court's decisions. The usual path by which a state case moves to the federal level is to go from the California Supreme Court to the U.S. Supreme Court, but it is possible for a case to bypass a state supreme court and go directly from a court of appeal to the U.S. Supreme Court.

What does that mean?

Litigate: to argue a claim or dispute in a court of law

Trial: formal legal process where the facts and law are examined before a court in order to determine an issue

Appeal: a legal proceeding by which a case is brought before a higher court for review of a decision made by a lower court

Appellate: having the power to hear court appeals and to review court decisions

Jurisdiction: the right and power to interpret and apply the law

Figure 6.1   **Federal & State Courts**

U.S. SUPREME

CHIEF JUSTICE

ASSOCIATE JUSTICES

final interpreter of the U.S. Constitution
justices appointed by the U.S. President, confirmed by the U.S. Senate
formal opinions given on 80-90 cases per term, out of over 10,000 on the docket

discretionary review

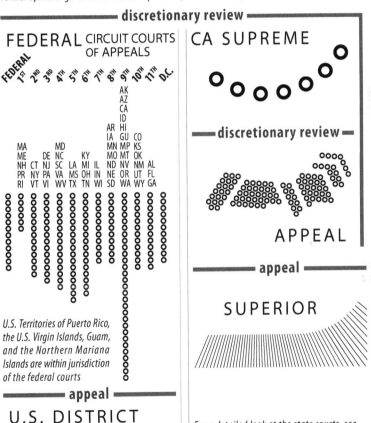

FEDERAL CIRCUIT COURTS OF APPEALS

FEDERAL 1ST 2ND 3RD 4TH 5TH 6TH 7TH 8TH 9TH 10TH 11TH D.C.

							AK		
							AZ		
							CA		
							ID		
						AR	HI		
						IA	GU	CO	
MA | MD | | | | | MN | MP | KS | |
ME | DE | NC | KY | | | MO | MT | OK | |
NH | CT | NJ | SC | LA | MI | IL | ND | NV | NM | AL
PR | NY | PA | VA | MS | OH | IN | NE | OR | UT | FL
RI | VT | VI | WV | TX | TN | WI | SD | WA | WY | GA

U.S. Territories of Puerto Rico, the U.S. Virgin Islands, Guam, and the Northern Mariana Islands are within jurisdiction of the federal courts

appeal

U.S. DISTRICT

Districts in California:

NORTHERN: SAN FRANCISCO AND SAN JOSE
EASTERN: SACRAMENTO AND FRESNO
CENTRAL: LOS ANGELES
SOUTHERN: SAN DIEGO

CA SUPREME

discretionary review

APPEAL

appeal

SUPERIOR

For a detailed look at the state courts, see Figure 6.2: The California Court System

If you want more background ...

The federal judicial structure, similar to California's, is a hierarchy of courts. There are thirteen federal circuit courts of appeals below the U.S. Supreme Court. The court of appeals for the federal circuit decides specialized federal cases, generally rising under patent, copyright, or customs laws, or involving disputes over contracts with the federal government. The other twelve circuits are regionally organized, and hear appeals from the federal district courts in their regions. For example, the U.S. Ninth Circuit Court of Appeals, headquartered in San Francisco, hears appeals from federal district courts located throughout California and several other Western states. California has four federal district courts: San Francisco and San Jose (northern district), Sacramento and Fresno (eastern district), Los Angeles (central dis¬trict), and San Diego (southern district).

CALIFORNIA COURTS

There are two basic types of California courts: trial and appellate. At the trial level, cases are "tried" in a superior court. A trial is a formal legal process whereby a court examines the facts and laws and a decision is made on the court's findings. The decision may be appealed to a higher (appellate) court to determine whether the proper procedures were used in the original trial, or whether the law was correctly applied or interpreted. Usually, the California Supreme Court and courts of appeal hear cases only on appeal.

Criminal and Civil Cases

California courts handle both criminal and civil cases.

A **criminal case** involves violation of a law for which a fine or other penalty is prescribed, and the violation is considered an offense against the state. There are three levels of crimes, increasing in seriousness:

- infractions – such as minor traffic offenses, punishable by a fine or community service
- misdemeanors – more serious crimes that have higher penalties, such as imprisonment in a county jail for less than one year
- felonies – crimes that are punishable by imprisonment in a state prison for a term of more than a year or, for capital cases, for capital cases, a crime that may be punishable by death

If the state believes an individual has committed a crime, it may file charges. In a criminal case, the prosecutor charges the defendant with an offense and, if a trial follows, has the burden of proving the charges. Generally, the district attorney's office acts as the prosecutor and represents the state, sometimes referred to as "the people." Each county has its own district attorney's office. Some offenses are prosecuted by a city attorney. In the courts of appeal and the Supreme Court, the California attorney general represents the state. Only the government, not another person or private agency, can charge an individual with a criminal violation.

More than 90 percent of cases in California are settled by a plea bargain and do not go to trial. In a plea bargain a defen- dant agrees to plead guilty in return for a reduced sentence or the dismissal of some charges.

The defendant in a criminal case is represented by a private attorney, public defender, or court-appointed attorney. In addition, defendants may be allowed to represent themselves as counsel (pro se) if the judge determines that the accused is competent. Criminal defendants are presumed innocent until proven guilty. In a criminal case, a jury must agree unanimously on the verdict, whether guilty or not guilty. If the jury cannot agree unanimously one way or the other, it is a "hung jury," and the judge must declare a mistrial. After a mistrial is declared, the case may be dropped or a new trial may be ordered.

Civil cases involve disputes between two or more parties (individuals, corporations, or groups) who wish to obtain a court ruling on non-criminal legal matters. Frequently, they are brought to recover damages for injury to persons or property, or to settle disputes over terms of a contract or over property rights. A plaintiff may sue to prevent an act (e.g., the cutting of certain timber) or to compel action (e.g., better street lighting in a specified neighborhood). If a civil trial is decided by a jury, a verdict is reached by agreement of three-fourths of the jurors. Examples of civil proceedings are probate of uncontested wills, dissolution of marriages, adoptions, and the appointment of guardians.

What does that mean?

Probate: the court process by which a will is proved valid or invalid

Plaintiff: A person who brings a case against someone in a court of law

---

Superior Courts

Before 1998, each county in California had municipal or justice courts that heard cases with "amounts in controversy," or the amount at stake in a lawsuit, below $25,000. In 1998, California voters adopted Proposition 220, a constitutional amendment that allowed the judges in each county to consolidate the municipal and superior courts into a single unified superior court. By 2001, every county in the state had consolidated its

Figure 6.2 **The California Court System**

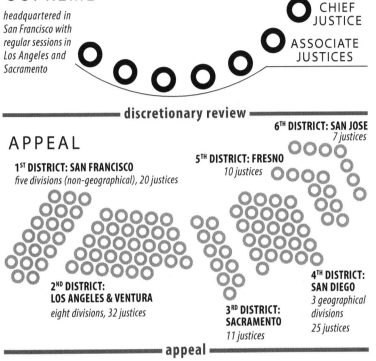

SUPREME

*headquartered in
San Francisco with
regular sessions in
Los Angeles and
Sacramento*

CHIEF
JUSTICE

ASSOCIATE
JUSTICES

discretionary review

APPEAL

1ST DISTRICT: SAN FRANCISCO
five divisions (non-geographical), 20 justices

**2ND DISTRICT:
LOS ANGELES & VENTURA**
eight divisions, 32 justices

5TH DISTRICT: FRESNO
10 justices

**3RD DISTRICT:
SACRAMENTO**
11 justices

6TH DISTRICT: SAN JOSE
7 justices

**4TH DISTRICT:
SAN DIEGO**
*3 geographical
divisions
25 justices*

appeal

SUPERIOR

58 trial courts, 1 for each county

number of judges per court determined by the Legislature

jurisdiction over all criminal cases and all civil cases

death penalty cases automatically appealed directly to the Supreme Court

MUNICIPAL COURTS   JUSTICE COURTS

*In 1998, California voters adopted **Proposition 220**, a constitutional amendment that allowed
the judges in each county to consolidate the municipal and superior courts into a single, unified
superior court. By 2001, consolidation of the lower courts of every county in the state was complete.*

lower courts into a single superior court. Superior courts have jurisdiction over all criminal cases, from infractions to felonies, and all civil cases, including family law, probate, juvenile, personal injury claims, and other general civil matters.

Currently, California has 58 trial courts, one in each county. The California Legislature determines the number of judges in each court. Superior court judges serve six-year terms, and are elected by county voters at a general election. The governor appoints a judge when there is a vacancy. Superior court judges must be admitted to practice law in California or have served as a judge for at least ten years immediately before election by voters or appointment by the governor.

Traffic citations? Find information and contacts at <courts.ca.gov/find-my-court.htm>.

At least one judge in each superior court sits as judge of the juvenile court, which hears cases concerning persons under 18 years of age. Regardless of the alleged offense, juvenile court proceedings are civil, not criminal. Both the proceedings and procedural safeguards for the juvenile differ somewhat from those for an accused adult. Instead of jury trials, for example, there are hearings before the juvenile judge. Routine cases are sometimes heard by court-appointed referees. Since 1982, a "fitness" hearing has been required before a youth over the age of 16 but under the age of 18 accused of a serious crime is treated as a juvenile instead of an adult.

An appeal from a superior court in a death penalty case must go directly to the California Supreme Court. Other appeals from superior courts go to the court of appeal for each area. Either party may appeal a superior court decision.

If you want more background ...

The California Legislature also determines the number and salaries of superior court judges. Legislation enacted in 1997 consolidated all court funding at the state level, giving the Legislature authority to appropriate funds and the Judicial Council responsibility to allocate funds. In addition, it transferred all future growth costs from the counties to the state, and the counties' financial responsibility was capped at the fiscal year 1994-95 level.

Courts of Appeal

Created by a constitutional amendment in 1904, California's courts of appeal review decisions appealed from superior courts. California has six appellate districts, three having multiple divisions. The district headquarters are in San Francisco (First Appellate); Los Angeles (Second Appellate); Sacramento (Third Appellate); San Diego (Fourth Appellate); Fresno (Fifth Appellate); and San Jose (Sixth Appellate). Each district has a presiding justice and two or more associate justices, appointed by the governor and confirmed by the Commission on Judicial Appointments.

Appellate court judges study the transcripts of testimony and documents from the original hearing, and attorneys present written briefs and oral arguments. The judges confer in private before voting. Two judges must agree in a decision. All decisions must be in writing. Approximately 12 percent of the decisions are selected for publication as precedent that lawyers may cite. The Supreme Court has discretion to order an opinion "de-published," which means it cannot be cited as a precedent. Appeals from decisions of the courts of appeal are sent to the California Supreme Court, which has authority to select cases to review. Most cases, however, go no higher than the courts of appeal.

The qualifications and selection of justices for the courts of appeal are the same as those for the California Supreme Court. The state assumes all costs of both courts.

The California Supreme Court

An individual or group that is dissatisfied with a decision made by a court of appeal may ask the California Supreme Court to review the issues, which is called a petition for review. Most petitions for review are denied; the Supreme Court accepts cases to decide important legal questions or to maintain uniformity in the law. Nonetheless, deciding which cases to review occupies a sizable portion of the Supreme Court justices' time. The California Supreme Court has the final word on the content and application of the law in the state. The United States Supreme Court may review a decision of the California Supreme Court only when it concerns an issue of federal law.

If you want more background ...

Since 1984, the California Supreme Court has been permitted to focus its review of an appeal on specified issues. Under previous practice, the Court could only review "all or nothing," meaning the Court had to review the whole case after a decision by a court of appeal, or let the Court of Appeal's decision stand in its entirety.

The California Supreme Court is required to hear capital cases. State law provides that a judgment sentencing a defendant to death must be appealed to the state Supreme Court. The defendant cannot waive the right to appeal.

The California Supreme Court has original jurisdiction in habeas corpus proceedings.

What does that mean?

Habeas corpus: the requirement to bring a person before a court or judge for a hearing, before being imprisoned.

It also has the power to:
- transfer to itself a case pending before a court of appeal

- transfer a case before the Supreme Court, other than a death penalty appeal, to a court of appeal
- transfer cases between courts of appeal

In addition, the California Supreme Court reviews recommendations from the Commission on Judicial Performance and the State Bar of California concerning the removal and suspension of judges and attorneys due to misconduct.

Members of the California Supreme Court include a chief justice and six associate justices. Four justices must agree in a judgment. Similar to courts of appeal justices, members of the Supreme Court are appointed by the governor and confirmed by the Commission on Judicial Appointments. To be considered for appointment, an individual must be an attorney admitted to practice law in California or have served as a judge of a court of record for ten years immediately preceding appointment. The state Constitution directs the chief justice to expedite the handling of judicial business and to equalize the work of judges. For this reason, judges from courts with light workloads may be assigned to those with congested calendars, and, with their consent, retired judges may be assigned to any court.

Further Background on the California Supreme Court

Supreme Court justices serve twelve-year terms, but a justice is frequently appointed to complete the term of his or her predecessor. Voters approve constitutional provisions affecting the selection of Supreme Court and courts of appeal justices. If an incumbent files for reelection, the governor makes no nomination. A candidate runs unopposed, and the ballot question is whether he or she shall be retained in office. For a Supreme Court justice the vote is statewide; for the courts of appeal, it is by district. If the candidate does not receive a majority affirmation, the governor appoints a different person to the office. Every appointee must receive voter affirmation at the first gubernatorial election following the appointment, in order to continue in office.

COMMISSION ON JUDICIAL APPOINTMENTS
<courts.ca.gov/5367.htm>

The Commission on Judicial Appointments consists of the California Chief Justice, the California Attorney General, and the Senior Presiding Justice of the Court of Appeal of the affected district. When a Supreme Court appointee is being considered, the third member of the commission is the state's senior presiding justice of the courts of appeal. The commission convenes after the governor nominates or appoints a person to fill a vacancy on either the California Supreme Court or a court of appeal. The commission holds one or more public hearings to review the appointee's qualifications and may confirm or veto the appointment. No appellate appointment is final until the commission has filed its approval with the Secretary of State.

JUDICIAL COUNCIL
<courts.ca.gov/policyadmin-jc.htm>

The Judicial Council is the policymaking body of the California courts. The council is responsible for ensuring the consistent, independent, impartial, and accessible administration of justice. The chief justice from the California Supreme Court, as chairperson, appoints 14 of its 21 members from judges of the Supreme Court, the courts of appeal, and the superior courts. Four attorneys are appointed by the state bar, and one member is appointed by each legislative house. The judges and attorneys serve two-year terms, while the legislative appointees' terms are determined in each house.

In order to improve the administration of justice, the Judicial Council continually surveys the business of all state courts, including the 18 divisions of the courts of appeal and the 58 superior courts. It makes recommendations to the governor, the Legislature, and the various courts, and it adopts and revises the California Rules of Court in the areas of court procedure, practice, and administration. For example, it devises rules regarding appeals, bail, photographing, broadcasting, and recording court proceedings. The council uploads videos of important court proceedings and other selected clips on its Web site. The council performs these functions with the support of its staff agency, the Administrative Office of the Courts.

Administrative Law Judges

Government agencies are created to deal with specific areas of public policy. For example, the California Environmental Protection Agency deals with protecting water and air from pollution and the Department of Motor Vehicles deals with safe operation of vehicles. Because agencies focus on limited areas, they are able to develop special expertise that a court would not have. Both federal and state agencies employ administrative law judges. An administrative law judge (ALJ) is an official who hears disputes arising from agency actions and other matters in the area regulated by the agency. In California, a few of the agencies that employ ALJs are:

- The California Department of Consumer Affairs
- The California Department of Health Care Services
- The California Department of Industrial Relations
- The California Department of Social Services
- The California Employment Development Department
- The California Public Utilities Commission

The Consumer Protection Agency began regulating medical practices in 1876. It now licenses more than 100 business and 200 professional categories.

Like trial court judges, ALJs hear cases that involve testimony and evidence-gathering. An ALJ's decision may first be appealed within the agency, for example to the Chief ALJ or to the appointed board or commissioners. A party may then file for review by an appellate court. For example, at the Public Utilities Commission, the governor appoints five commissioners who vote to adopt or reject ALJ decisions.

Unlike superior court judges or court of appeal justices, ALJs are not elected or appointed. Within an agency, a Chief ALJ may be appointed to manage the ALJ division. While most ALJs are lawyers, others are experts with technical experience relevant to the agency's practice. For example, many ALJs in the Public Utilities Commission have technical backgrounds that help them interpret complex utility data.

For agencies without an ALJ division, the Office of Administrative Hearings may provide an ALJ. Established by the California Legislature in 1945, the Office of Administrative Hearings provides ALJs to over 1,400 state and local government agencies. These ALJs are fully independent of the agencies and adjudicate and provide alternative dispute resolution opportunities. If there is a dispute between an action proposed by a governmental agency and an individual or business, a hearing before the Office of Administrative Hearings may be requested.

Alternative Dispute Resolution. Alternative dispute resolution aims at resolving cases before they proceed to trial. There are several methods of alternative dispute resolution, including negotiation and settlement, and mediation.

You can resolve your dispute out of court. Use ADR resources for civil cases: <courts.ca.gov/3075.htm>.

In negotiation, attorneys acting on behalf of their clients settle differences by reaching a compromise or agreement. This process requires that an attorney advocate on behalf of the client, and the bargaining process often requires concessions by all parties. As the vast majority of cases in the United States are settled before reaching trial, this process is effective and can save both time and money.

Mediation is an informal, confidential process where a neutral person, the mediator, helps parties reach their own acceptable and voluntary agreement. The mediator encourages the parties but does not dictate the end result.

State Bar

The State Bar of California is a public corporation to which all attorneys licensed to practice law in California must belong.

The State Bar's Board of Governors rules on qualifications for practicing law. The Committee of Bar Examiners reviews candidates and recommends qualified applicants to the California Supreme Court, which grants formal admission to the bar. The State Bar also recommends disciplinary actions concerning attorneys to the Supreme Court. For more information: <courts.ca.gov/3016.htm>.

Discipline and Removal of Judges

The California Constitution contains specific provisions for disciplining judges. A judge is disqualified from acting as a judge, without loss of salary, if charged with a felony or while the Supreme Court is considering a recommendation for the judge's removal or retirement. A judge must be removed if convicted of a felony or a serious vicious crime, and during appeal he or she may be suspended without pay. The California Supreme Court decides if disciplinary action is appropriate in other situations, but it may act only on recommendations from the Commission on Judicial Performance.

The Commission on Judicial Performance investigates and may hold hearings on charges against any California judge. If the judge's conduct does not warrant formal proceedings, the commission may reprimand the judge privately. All judges are subject to recall and impeachment. There is no mandatory retirement age, but the state's contributory pension plan for judges offers some inducement to retire at age seventy. In addition, the Supreme Court may retire a judge because of serious disability, or may censure or remove a judge for failure to perform duties, habitual intemperate use of drugs or intoxicants, misconduct in office, or conduct that "brings the judicial office into disrepute." A judge removed by the court is ineligible for subsequent judicial office and, pending further order of the Supreme Court, is suspended from practicing law in the state.

JURIES

In many legal cases a jury, a panel of ordinary citizens, is tasked with judging the guilt or innocence of an accused party. While the judge gives direction to the jury and decides the final sentence, if any, the jury evaluates the facts, evidence, and credibility of witnesses and pronounces the verdict in accordance with the rules given by the trial judge.

A **trial jury** (*petit jury*) consists of 12 persons, referred to as jurors, although the Legislature may provide for eight-person juries in civil cases in superior courts. Jurors are randomly selected from lists of registered voters, licensed drivers, public utility users, and others. To serve as a juror, a person must

- be a U.S. citizen
- be at least 18 years of age
- understand English
- live within the court's jurisdiction
- not have been convicted of a felony or malfeasance while in public office
- not be on active military duty
- not be serving on a grand jury or another trial jury

A person may be excused from jury duty if it causes undue hardship to that person or to the public he or she serves. A jury trial may be waived in either a civil or criminal case if both parties agree. If there is no jury, the judge makes the decision. According to the California Supreme Court, and under the California Constitution, the right to a jury trial cannot be waived in an agreement before any court proceeding has begun.

A **grand jury** of 19 citizens (23 in Los Angeles County) must be summoned in each county every year. The superior court judges of each county nominate these jurors, and jurors are selected from their nominations. The responsibilities of grand juries include examining matters of county government, such as the condition of jails, activities of public officials, records and accounts of agencies, and the efficiency of government operations. Grand juries may recommend creating new county offices or abolishing existing ones. They handle citizen complaints on matters concerning county government. In addition, grand juries may issue criminal indictments that require defendants to go on trial on felony charges. When there is reason to believe a crime may have been committed, the grand jury may, at the request of the district attorney, hear witnesses and determine if the evidence is sufficient to warrant a trial. If so, it returns to the court an indictment of the accused. Grand juries spend considerably more time on investigating and reporting on government operations than they do on criminal matters. They are not limited in their choice of subjects or depth of inquiry except by their one-year terms of office. At the end of the investigation, the jury submits a final report containing specific recommendations to the board of supervisors.

13 languages are certified for court interpreters.

Some counties have two grand juries: one that functions as a governmental watchdog, and the other that returns criminal indictments.

A **coroner's jury** (jury of inquest) of 6 to 15 persons may be summoned by the coroner to hear testimony in cases of death in unusual circumstances, or when violence, suicide, or criminal activity is suspected. The jury's role is to determine whether further action is necessary.

LEGAL SERVICES

In California, several federal and state agencies provide legal assistance for people who cannot afford lawyers.

- A low-income defendant in a criminal case may be represented by either a public defender or a private lawyer appointed by the court. More than half of the people accused of serious crimes in California use public defenders or court-appointed counsel.

- County public defenders represent their clients in the trial courts. Many counties in the state either have a public defender's office or contract with the state to handle cases for low-income defendants. Other counties provide defense attorneys via court appointment on a case-by-case basis through annual contracts with a county bar association.
- The Office of the State Public Defender provides legal representation for low-income people before the California Supreme Court and the courts of appeal. The state public defender is appointed by the governor for a minimum term of four years and is authorized to contract with county public defenders, private attorneys, and others to provide legal services.

California has a variety of federal and state programs that provide legal aid in civil cases. For example, the federal Legal Services Corporation provides federal funds for neighborhood legal offices that offer assistance in civil actions such as divorces, property damage, personal injuries, contracts, and bankruptcies. In addition, the State Bar of California Website lists by county lawyer referral services that refer potential clients to attorneys. The state has a variety of programs that provide free civil legal services to low-income Californians. The Justice Gap Fund supports nonprofit organizations that enlist volunteer attorneys, law students and social service experts to expand legal-aid resources. Other groups include California Rural Legal Assistance and California Indian Legal Services. Federal funds also support the Western Center on Law and Poverty which recruits and trains poverty-law attorneys and files class action lawsuits on special legal problems of the poor. Most law schools in California offer free (*pro bono*) legal services by coordinating with local attorneys.

Find free or low cost legal assistance and information at the California Courts self-help centers: <courts.ca.gov/selfhelp.htm>.

Working with Other Levels of Government

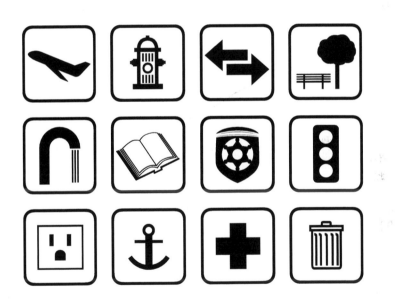

PART III

County Government

In many of their day-to-day activities, California citizens deal with county governments rather than directly with the state. Counties are geographical and political subdivisions of the state and they serve as important administrative units for state and federal laws, programs and services. Some of the functions of counties are to:

- build roads
- maintain jails
- care for the poor
- enforce laws in unincorporated areas
- keep property records
- maintain statistics on residents

More than fifty five percent of county revenues come from the state or federal government. Because counties function as agents of state government, they are subject to extensive state supervision and regulation. The state may delegate or take back any of the functions that belong to the state. Unlike city governments, counties lack the power to generate revenues, although they do have some local autonomy. County government is in the hands of local elected officials responsible to local citizens. These officials deal with needs, wants and resources which differ greatly from county to county.

Structure of County Government

California's 58 counties vary greatly in size, geography and population. San Bernardino County, the largest in area, is 46 times as large as Santa Cruz County, the smallest except for the combined city-county of San Francisco. The population of Los Angeles County is nearly ten million, while that of Alpine County is just over 1,000. Because of these differences, state law grants broad discretionary powers. Counties may adapt their internal structure, operations and programs to local conditions.

Over the years there have been some changes in the boundaries of counties. During the state's first 60 years, the original 27 counties of 1850 became 58. Although legally possible, forming a new county is politically difficult. The state Constitution requires that formation of a new county must be approved by a majority of those voting on the question in each county concerned.

Santa Clara County is the fastest growing county in the state (1.6 percent from 1/2012 to 1/2013).

General Law and Charter Counties

The state Constitution provides for three classes of county government:

- general law
- charter
- consolidated city and county (which must be a charter unit)

The main difference between general law and charter counties lies in the way they can organize and select their county governing bodies and officers. The procedures for adopting or amending county charters are the same as for city charters

Figure 7.1

California Counties

TEN MOST POPULOUS 2010

Los Angeles	9,818,605
San Diego	3,095,313
Orange	3,010,232
Riverside	2,189,641
San Bernardino	2,035,210
Santa Clara	1,781,642
Alameda	1,510,271
Sacramento	1,418,788
Contra Costa	1,049,025
Fresno	930,450

LEAST POPULOUS

Alpine	1,175

TEN LARGEST (sq. miles)

San Bernardino	20,164
Inyo	10,097
Kern	8,170
Riverside	7,243
Siskiyou	6,318
Fresno	5,998
Tulare	4,844
Lassen	4,690
Imperial	4,598
Modoc	4,340

SMALLEST

San Francisco	91

Population figures from the 2010 U.S. Census

(See Chapter 8.) Every county is required to elect a governing body—a board of supervisors.

General law counties elect supervisors by district. Every county must elect a sheriff, district attorney, and assessor. Although general law counties have been granted some flexibility, they do not have the latitude of charter counties regarding officers. General law counties are regulated by statutes that specify their principal officers, assign their duties and require that they be elected by the people. The law, however, permits boards of supervisors to consolidate these elective offices into any of 25 combinations and to appoint additional officers, but prohibits the supervisors from giving appointed officials the responsibilities assigned by law to elected officials.

Charter counties have the option of electing supervisors at large or by district. They must elect a sheriff, district attorney, and assessor, but have considerable freedom when drafting their charters to determine what other officers they will have, their powers and duties, and whether they will be elected or appointed.

Functions of County Government Policymaking

California counties have five supervisors elected for four-year staggered terms on a nonpartisan ballot, except for the city-county of San Francisco, which has 11 supervisors and a mayor. If a supervisorial position becomes vacant between elections, it is filled by the governor in general law counties. Charter counties may make other provisions for filling vacancies. In all counties, supervisorial district boundaries must be adjusted after each federal census so that the population of each of their districts is as nearly equal to each other as possible.

The board of supervisors is the legislative and executive body of county government. The supervisors pass all ordinances governing the county and are responsible for seeing that functions delegated to the county are properly discharged. Among their

tasks are the following:
- adopting the budget
- setting employee salaries
- determining personnel matters when there is no independent personnel board or civil service system
- supervising public works, including the county road system
- serving in ex-officio capacity as the board of directors for special districts of various kinds
- representing their counties on councils of government (COGs) and other regional bodies.

The board of supervisors has responsibility for overseeing a variety of services to county residents, including those in cities as well as those in unincorporated areas. Such county-wide services include voter registration; health and welfare programs; court and law enforcement operations; jail facilities; the recording of official documents, including vital statistics and real property transactions; tax assessment and collection; and social services.

The supervisors are also responsible for providing some municipal-type services for residents of unincorporated areas. These include planning, zoning, and land-use regulation; street maintenance; and in some cases sewage disposal, water, parks and recreational facilities, and other municipal services. Policy decisions on the degree of service lie with the board of supervisors. Highly urbanized unincorporated areas may have the same service needs as conventional cities. These needs are frequently met by formation of special districts.

The board of supervisors also has some quasi-judicial functions. For example, in many counties supervisors serve as the tax assessment appeals board and as the planning and land-use appeal body.

More information about California's counties may be found on the California County website <ca.gov/about/government/local/counties/index.html>.

Alpine, Mariposa, and Trinity counties contain no incorporated cities.

Administration of Counties

A **chief administrative officer** is appointed by the board of supervisors in most of the counties in the state. This officer is responsible for implementing board decisions, preparing the county budget, carrying out studies to provide the supervisors with information needed in making decisions, and generally coordinating county administration. Although the county officer is often called "county manager" or "county executive," there is a legal distinction. Only charter counties may establish the position of county manager or executive, and in these cases the officer has more authority than a chief administrative officer, who is essentially the agent of the board of supervisors.

Historically, the **county clerk** serves as the registrar of voters, ex-officio clerk of the board of supervisors, and ex officio clerk of the Superior Court and performs a variety of other functions such as issuing marriage licenses, processing passport applications and filing fictitious business names. In some counties, all of these functions have been retained by a single county officer; in others, the functions have been split into two or more offices.

The **county recorder** keeps records of births, deaths, marriages, all instruments recording real property, and other documents required by law. In some counties, this office is combined with that of the county clerk.

A **county counsel** may be appointed by the supervisors to serve as chief legal adviser on civil matters for the county. The counsel may discharge the civil duties of the district attorney, advise county officials on their responsibilities, and serve as attorney for them in their official capacity.

By charter or by ordinance approved by the electorate, a county may adopt a civil service system administered by an independent personnel board. Most counties have some form of civil service covering most of the non-elected personnel. Some counties arrange with the state Personnel Board for merit system assistance. All counties provide some kind of retirement plan for officials and employees, either by contract with the Public Employees' Retirement System or through an independent retirement system.

The **public administrator** is responsible for the administration of the estates of persons deceased without apparent heirs. On appointment by the court, the public administrator serves as guardian for people – often minors or the elderly – who are not competent to manage their affairs and lack private assistance.

FINANCE

Counties have four major financial officers:

- auditor or director of finance: monitors the financial records of all county departments, reports on the state of the county's finances and authorizes expenditures by warrants
- treasurer: custodian of the county's money, pays county obligations on warrant from the auditor, assists in the collection of taxes
- assessor: appraises property in the county that is subject to taxation
- tax collector: collects all county taxes and deposits them with the treasurer

County Revenues

Of total revenues received and collected by county governments, 90 percent can be classified into five distinct categories:

- state government 31 percent
- property taxes 21 percent
- federal government 17 percent
- enterprise receipts 13 percent
- current services 8 percent

The balance is made up of a variety of revenue sources.

Planning

Every county must have a planning agency. State law allows the supervisors to appoint "area planning commissions" to plan and regulate land use within distinct communities. The planning commission prepares and maintains a general plan for physical development of the county and reviews development plans for environmental impact. The commission is advisory to the supervisors, who approve and implement recommendations and hear appeals in disputes between citizens and the commission.

A local agency formation commission (LAFCo) is also required, although it is not a county body but an independent commission consisting of representatives from the county, cities and the general public. In some counties, special districts also sit on LAFCo. Proposals for boundary changes, such as municipal incorporation and annexation and formation or dissolution of independent special districts, require LAFCo approval. LAFCos must also adapt long-range service plans called "spheres of influence" for each city and special district in their county.

Law Enforcement

Sheriffs are the chief law enforcement officers in all unincorporated territory. The sheriff arrests people who violate the law, and may be in charge of the jail and other custodial facilities. Other duties include implementing programs to prevent crime, reduce delinquency and rehabilitate criminals.

The **district attorney** is the public prosecutor and in counties without a county counsel performs the counsel's duties as well. The district attorney prosecutes those accused of crimes and presents evidence of crime to the grand jury.

A **public defender** is appointed or contracted for in most counties to defend people who are charged with offenses but unable to pay for attorney services. The defender may bring civil cases on behalf of low-income people for claims not over $100 or defend them in civil suits if no other legal aid is available.

The **coroner** investigates causes of deaths occurring without medical attention under violent or unusual circumstances. When the cause of death is uncertain, a coroner's jury may be called to decide whether further action is warranted.

The **chief probation officer** is responsible for monitoring persons placed on probation by the courts. In addition, the probation department may have the responsibility of administering one or more alternative sentencing programs, such as home detention.

Every county has a **Superior Court** which has jurisdiction over all criminal and civil cases including felonies, misdemeanors, and traffic matters. They also have jurisdiction over all civil cases including family law, probate, juvenile, and general civil matters. Almost 8.5 million cases were filed in California during 2010-2011. The California Legislature determines the number of judges in each court. The number varies depending on population; there are 1,662 authorized judges for the entire state.

For further information about the court system, see Chapter 6 and also the California Judicial Branch Web site <courts.ca.gov/home.htm>.

Probation is a court-ordered period of supervision over an offender, either instead of prison time or after a prisoner has been released on parole.

Public Health

Counties provide medical services for people who cannot afford to pay for them. The system of poverty-based medical care varies from county to county and may involve county hospitals and clinics, contracts with private hospitals and clinics, or a mixture of both public and private facilities. Some small counties contract with the state to provide medical care services in a system similar to Medi-Cal.

County public health departments provide an array of services for people of all ages:

- emergency medical services
- infectious disease control
- immunizations
- public health labs

- drug and alcohol abuse prevention/intervention/treatment
- tobacco education
- child health screenings/treatment
- dental services
- home health services
- family planning
- prenatal services
- special services for seniors
- AIDS testing and counseling
- education and vital statistics

Environmental health, air pollution control and animal control are county responsibilities and may be included in the health department.

Welfare

County supervisors manage the welfare programs required by state and federal law. Forty percent of county expenditures each year are used for public assistance. County welfare depart¬ments administer programs overseen by the state Health and Human Services Agency. These departments determine eligibility and benefits in the California CalWORKS (TANF), Medi-Cal and CalFresh (food stamps) programs. County welfare departments also deliver social services to eligible persons in need of child care, family planning, health, and homemaker services. They offer protective services to adults and children and are required to provide such services as foster care to children in danger of abuse and exploitation. Welfare departments license care facilities and provide information and referral to anyone regardless of eligibility. Some counties also provide emergency housing, legal assistance, suste¬nance programs, and adoption services.

 All counties are required to administer a general relief program that gives financial aid to needy individuals who are not served by established state and federal programs. Counties receive federal and state funds for support of many programs but each county must fund its own general-relief program.

Public Works
Some counties employ a director of public works to assume responsibility for county buildings, roads, solid waste disposal and other physical facilities such as sewage treatment or flood control and drainage projects. A county surveyor conducts surveys, where necessary, of the condition of old and new monuments in the county, keeps survey records, and supplies copies of maps required by the recorder's office. In some counties, the surveyor is also the county engineer. This office may also include building inspection.

Libraries

County boards of supervisors establish and maintain free public libraries and appoint county librarians. These libraries may be administered as a special district or as a general fund department of county government. Funding for library operation comes from local property taxes and allocations from the state budget's public library fund. City libraries may exist as separate and independent institutions within the county or the city, and county libraries may function as a consolidated system. Most public libraries belong to a statewide cooperative system to share resources and provide services.

City and county library systems serve more than 90 percent of California residents, with each type of library seving about 45 percent. JPA (Joint Powers of Authority) and special district libraries provide services to 7.27 percent and 1.36 percent, respectively.

Other Offices
There is some flexibility in the way counties administer their services. In most counties, for example, the county clerk is an elected nonpartisan officer, but some large counties appoint their county clerks. Many counties now have information technology officers, but several do not. Some county offices are not required in all counties:

See Figure 7.1 on next page.

For further information about counties, go to the California State Association of Counties website <csac.counties.org/>.

Figure 7.2   **Optional County Offices**

REQUIRED FOR GENERAL LAW COUNTIES, DISCRETIONARY FOR CHARTER COUNTIES	NOT REQUIRED, OFTEN IN PLACE
fire marshal	agricultural commissioner
livestock inspector	health officer
sealer of weights and measures	public guardian
	information technology officer

INTERGOVERNMENTAL COOPERATION

More people live in California, an estimated 38.8 million of them in 2014, than in any other state in America. About 75 percent of Californians live in the metropolitan areas surrounding Los Angeles, the San Francisco Bay Area, and Riverside-San Bernardino counties. This concentrated population has resulted in fragmented land-use planning, traffic congestion, and environmental deterioration. In the absence of enforceable area-wide planning, important decisions on land use and governmental policy can be made by many separate and unrelated governmental units. Intergovernmental cooperation (among cities, counties, schools, special districts, regional agencies, and the state) is necessary for the balancing of interests, the efficient provision of services, and agreement on long-term solutions in the best interests of the total region. Yet such cooperation can be difficult to achieve. California has developed a number of approaches to cooperation, including the Joint Exercise of Powers Act and legislation establishing regional organizations with considerable authority.

The California Association of Councils of Government <calcog. org/> provides a way for local governmental agencies to work together to make state government run more efficiently. Its Web site identifies the focus areas the group has chosen. Here is a slightly abbreviated version of its list:

1. **Peer-to-Peer Learning**: CALCOG facilitates information exchanges between members. Although each region is unique, members can learn from one another's experiences, share information, and build each other's capacity. This type of exchange leads to better policy outcomes.

2. **Partnership with CalTrans and California Transportation Commission**: California is a leader in incorporating local decision-making into the planning, funding, and delivery of the transportation networks. The state's Metropolitan Planning Organizations and Regional Transportation Planning Agencies allocate 75 percent of the funds for the Surface Transportation Program, Congestion Mitigation and Air Quality Improvement Program, and State Transportation Improvement Program. But with this duty comes a responsibility to work with the state to assure that state goals are met. CALCOG facilitates this partnership by monitoring developments on behalf of members, and facilitating policy discussion forums between state, regional, and local officials.

3. **Transportation Financing**: CALCOG members have extensive knowledge of transportation needs and the chronic lack of funding to address those needs. CALCOG members worked with the California Transportation Commission to develop a comprehensive statewide needs assessment for the entire transportation and goods movement system. CALCOG works with organizations to educate decision makers and stake-holders regarding the needs, revenue options, and impacts and analysis, of different financing structures.

4. **The (Not So) New World of Planning**: Under Senate Bill 375, Metropolitan Planning Organizations (MPOs) must develop regional transportation plans that take

into account how land use decisions may affect the needs of the transportation system. CALCOG continues to work with state agencies to ensure that there are adequate financial resources in place for regional and local agencies, not only to make plans, but to bring those plans to life.

What does that mean?

SB 375, signed into law in 2008, calls upon each of California's 18 regions to develop an **integrated transportation, land-use, and housing plan** known as a Sustainable Communities Strategy. This plan must demonstrate how the region will reduce greenhouse gas emissions through long-range planning. The purpose is to reduce the amount of driving people have to do and therefore reduce greenhouse gas emissions.

For more information: <sf-planning.org/index. aspx?page=2655>.

Explainer of Things COG: Many people, including state officials, public and private interest groups, and even other local officials do not always understand what COGs do and how they function. CALCOG explains the basics of how voluntary regional collaboration leads to greater efficiencies and better planning and service delivery. Everyone is their audience, including local, state, and federal officials; academia; business; and nonprofit sector organizations.

Monitor State Legislation: CALCOG monitors state legislation related to transportation, housing, environmental quality, land use, and planning. It presents these to the membership through COG director meetings in order to determine the positions of member agencies and whether it is useful, appropriate, or necessary for CALCOG to serve as a facilitator to resolve differences or to comment on the potential impact of a bill or administrative action.

State Agency Point of Contact and Collaborator: CALCOG collaborates, educates, and shares information with several state agencies as they develop policy that relates to regional planning issues. These agencies include, among others, the Department of Housing and Community Development, Air Resources Board, Strategic Growth Council, and the Governor's Office of Planning and Research.

Collaboration on Federal Transportation Policy: CALCOG collaborates with CALTRANS; the Business, Transportation, and Housing Agency; and the California Transportation Commission to develop a statewide unified position on federal transportation issues.

COG Governance Capacity: Finally, CALCOG members are all public organizations striving to deliver high-quality, cost-effective services to their own member local governments and the public they serve. There are commonalities in organizational responsibilities, in terms of board education, communicating with the public, staffing, and general governance issues that affect the overall effectiveness of the organization. CALCOG was started to identify materials and facilitate programs where members can explore these issues to help improve the capacity of its individual members.

Municipal Advisory Councils

A Municipal Advisory Council is an advisory body of local citizens elected by the community or appointed by the board of supervisors with the purpose of representing the community to the board. They grew out of the need by unincorporated communities for increased influence with their county boards of supervisors, and were authorized by a 1971 legislative statute. Although a municipal advisory council is a governing body, it has no fiscal authority or administrative organization. Because it lacks authority to implement its position directly, it seeks to accomplish its goals through county government.

These councils face two ways: toward the county, offering the views of the community; and toward the community, supplying information about county proposals and a place where individuals can air opinions on community problems and perhaps receive help. Activities of these councils include:

- public meetings
- community surveys
- representation of community to the board of supervisors.

The most common subject addressed in these activities is land-use planning. The county often uses the group as a planning advisory council to draft or revise the community's portion of the county general plan.

City Government CHAPTER 8

<cacities.org>

City governments provide many of the local services that affect our daily lives. Depending on the size of the city, these services usually include:

- police protection
- fire protection
- health services such as clinics and hospitals
- construction and maintenance of streets, sewers, and storm systems
- waste disposal
- public transportation
- park and other recreational facilities
- water systems and sometimes other municipal utilities such as gas and electricity
- city and environmental planning

POWERS AND STRUCTURE OF CITY GOVERNMENT

Cities are granted their powers by the state and the laws and regulations they impose must not be in conflict with state or federal law.

City governments: have the power

- to protect the health, safety, and welfare of their people
- to raise money by imposing taxes, license, and service fees, and by borrowing
- to employ needed personnel
- to condemn property for public use

Cities are created only by the request and consent of the residents in a given area. Communities may incorporate as cities for many reasons – to control population growth and development, to gain local control of tax money, to provide services, to promote special interests, to solve specific problems, to offer a more responsive unit of government, or to prevent annexation to adjoining cities.

All California cities are municipal corporations. Their formation is provided for in the state Constitution, and they fall into three categories:

- general law cities (361)
- charter cities (121)
- one consolidated city and county (San Francisco)

Information and news about cities are available from the League of California Cities <cacities.org/Home>.

General Law and Charter Cities

General Law cities derive their powers from and organize their governments according to acts of the Legislature. The fundamental law of these cities is found in the California Government Code, which spells out their powers and specifies their structure. The full text of the code is available at <leginfo.legislature.ca.gov/faces/codes.xhtml>.

Charter cities are formed when citizens specifically frame and adopt a charter or document to establish the organization and basic law of the city. The Constitution guarantees to these charter cities a large measure of "home rule," granting to them, direct control over local affairs, independent of the Legislature.

The basic difference between general law and charter cities is the extent to which they are controlled by the state government. Charter cities have more freedom to innovate and to pass ordinances according to local need. General law cities, nevertheless, have considerable choice in their form of municipal government and fairly broad powers over local affairs. Because the Legislature has tended to give general law cities the same control over internal matters that the Constitution grants to charter cities, the original distinction between the two forms of city authority has blurred.

The smallest city in California is Vernon: population 112

Coordination of Local Governments and Agencies

Starting in 1963, California encouraged the creation of Local Agency Formation Commissions (LAFCos) in counties across the state. Today every county in California has a LAFCo. These perform an important function in regulating the jurisdictional and service boundaries of local governments and agencies.

If You Want To Know More ...

What is a LAFCo?

The Cortese-Knox-Hertzberg Local Government Reorganization Act of 2000 governs the structure and activities of **Local Agency Formation Commissions**.

Objectives

1. to encourage the orderly formation of local governmental agencies
2. to preserve agricultural land resources
3. to discourage urban sprawl

Composition

Composition varies from county to county. Almost all LAFCos are composed of two members from the board of supervisors and two members from the city councils in the county. Many also have two members from special districts in the county. These members select a representative from the general public. There are also alternate members for each agency. Every agency that is included in the LAFCo shares some of the cost.

Responsibilities

LAFCos are responsible for coordinating logical and timely changes in local government boundaries, conducting special studies of government functions, and seeing that services are provided efficiently and economically.

Authority

LAFCos regulate boundary changes, determine spheres of influence for all local governmental agencies, conduct service reviews of local agency and municipal services, initiate special district consolidations; and approve or disapprove contracts to provide services outside of an agency's boundary. LAFCOS must act in accordance with locally adopted policies.

Public Involvement

Citizens are welcome and encouraged to attend LAFCo meetings and state their views.

More information is available from the California Association of LAFCos <calafco.org/about.htm>.

Determination of City Boundaries

A county board of supervisors may initiate the incorporation of a city, or a group of citizens may do this by petition. The petition must be signed by at least 25 percent of the locally registered voters. A petition by landowners is possible, but rare. The petition is then submitted to the Local Agency Formation

Commission, which reviews the proposed plan for incorporation (a feasibility study of boundaries, service provision, and potential revenues), conducts a hearing, and then, frequently after suggesting changes, approves or denies the proposal.

If the petition is approved, the board of supervisors conducts a hearing to determine whether the procedure will continue:

1. If a majority of the voters file written protests, the board must terminate the procedures.
2. If there is no majority protest, the board must call an election.
3. The incorporation must be approved by a majority of the voters living within the proposed city.
4. If the vote is against incorporation, no proceedings to incorporate any of the same territory may be started for another two years.

After incorporation, a city may adopt a charter by following these steps:

1. An initiative petition, or the governing body, may call for an election to determine whether to draft or revise the charter.
2. The community elects a charter commission or allows the governing body to serve as the commission.
3. After the charter has been drafted, it must be approved by majority vote of the electorate.

4. Amendment or repeal of a charter may be proposed either by the city council or by initiative, and adopted by majority vote of the electorate.

A city may also disincorporate by following legislative procedures, although none has done so since 1972.

The first city to incorporate was Sacramento on February 27, 1850, while the most recent was Jurupa Valley on July 1, 2011.

If you want more details ...

Annexation and consolidation procedures parallel those for incorporation. Any land area contiguous to a city in the same county may be annexed to the city if such annexation does not result in an island of unincorporated land completely surrounded by the city or in narrow strips of unincorporated land. (Because earlier law did not prohibit them, such islands currently exist in some cities.) In rare cases, LAFCo can make an exception.

Proponents of an annexation must have the approval of LAFCo and the governing body. In inhabited territory (with at least 12 voters), a petition signed by 25 percent of the qualified voters is filed with LAFCo. If LAFCo approves, the city council calls a public hearing. If there is a protest, a special election is called. Annexation requires majority approval within the annexation area. Proposals for annexing uninhabited territory may be initiated by either the annexing city or the owners of the land. No election is held. If approved by LAFCo, the annexation occurs automatically, unless a protest is made by fifty percent or more of the owners of land and improvements in the area. A city cannot decline an annexation approved by LAFCo and not sufficiently protested, unless the annexation is very large relative to the city. Then an election is required.

Two or more cities may consolidate, but a city may not be annexed by, or consolidated with, another without majority approval of voters of both cities.

FUNCTIONS OF CITY GOVERNMENT

The basic functions of city government include policymaking, administration, and planning.

Policymaking

All cities in California are governed by an elected group (city council), which decides municipal policy and is responsible for

The largest city in California is Los Angeles, with a population of 3,862,839.

enacting and enforcing local laws. Council members may be elected at large or by district. In charter cities members may be nominated and elected in any manner stated in the charter. All city elections are nonpartisan. In most cities, except for very large ones, the council members and the mayor are part-time positions. The Constitution gives the voters in all cities the right to exercise the initiative and referendum, and to recall elected officers. Meetings of city councils and commissions or other advisory bodies must be open to the public.

Aside from LA, the only other California city with a population of more than a million is San Diego: population 1,355,896

In general law cities, a council of five, seven, or nine members is elected for four-year staggered terms. If the mayor is elected directly instead of being chosen by fellow council members, the term of office is two or four years, as determined by popular vote. The city clerk and treasurer also serve four-year terms. The chief of police and other department-level heads are appointed by the city council or the city manager under merit system procedures.

Charter cities, exhibit great variety in organization, being free to make any desired allocation of duties, powers, and functions between elective and appointive city officers. Charters may also provide for sub-governments in all or part of a city.

San Francisco is the only California city which is also a county.

Administration

Two forms of administrative organization exist in California cities: the council-manager system and the mayor-council system. These basic forms provide varied patterns of city government.

Council-manager. Most California cities have some form of centralized professional administration. The administrator may be called a city manager, city administrator, or chief administrative officer. Under this type of administration, the elected council provides political leadership and makes policy, while a full-time professional manager directs city departments in carrying out that policy.

Mayor-council. In some cities, usually small general law communities, the mayor is chosen from among the council members and is merely the council's presiding officer and the city's ceremonial head. The council has substantial administrative as well as legislative power, with all department heads reporting directly to the council. This is the weak-mayor system.

Strong-mayor. A number of cities, usually very large ones, use the strong-mayor system, though their charters set limits on how strong the mayor can be. In these cases, the mayor is directly elected by the people. A chief administrative officer or general manager is in most matters responsible directly to the mayor, but may not be removed without the consent of the council. Top-level authority over some matters may be vested in independent boards or in elected officials. Under this system, the extent of the mayor's administrative power depends in large part on his or her ability to elicit cooperation.

The population of San Jose is expected to exceed one million when the 2020 census is taken.

Planning

Most cities establish municipal planning agencies; these consist of a planning commission, the city council, a professional planning department, or a combination. All California cities must develop a general plan, consider environmental impact reports, and periodically review their capital improvements program.

The planning commission has major responsibility for adoption and administration of zoning laws, although a special board of zoning adjustment or an administrator may decide, subject to council review, on applications for conditional use or for variance from zoning requirements. Otherwise the planning commission itself acts on these matters, subject to council approval.

While the planning commission may also be concerned with the city's building regulations, sometimes a separate building commission formulates local building standards and approves applications for building permits. In some large cities, such as Los Angeles, members of the Public Works Commission are the only full-time paid commissioners.

Renewal projects to clear and rebuild or rehabilitate blighted areas are determined locally, but state law details the procedures to be used. Until 2012, most cities established redevelopment agencies to oversee these projects, but these agencies were dissolved in 2012 by state law. Changes in the ways cities handle rehabilitation agency work will be covered on the California Cities Web site <cacities.org/>.

Boards and Commissions

Various city boards and commissions oversee many city functions. Most of these units are advisory to the city council, but some have quasi-judicial or limited administrative powers. Some city charters specifically establish citizen boards as part of the city administration, with independent authority and control of funds in their areas of operation.

Advisory boards or committees may be established by special ordinance, with their tasks reflecting community concerns. These bodies gather information on issues, hear arguments, weigh values, and recommend action to the council. Such boards may be permanent or may be assigned only one specific task. Except in very small communities, permanent commissions usually have the assistance of professional and clerical staff.

Besides the planning commission, cities frequently have several other boards:

1. A civil service or personnel board sets or recommends policy on employee compensation and working conditions, subject to state law. It hears appeals and grievances relating to city employment. A personnel director who works with the commission usually administers a merit system for hiring and promotions.

2. A human rights commission promotes understanding among racial, religious, and age groups.

3. Other boards that may be formed are a parks and recreation commission, youth board, a solid waste management board, a traffic commission, an airport or

Santa Clarita is at 15.4 percent 1/2012 to 1/2013.

harbor commission (which also has responsibilities supervised by the federal government), or an art or historical commission.

Although these bodies are advisory and vary greatly in size, funding, and powers, they often have great influence; a few have subpoena and hearing powers.

Harbor and airport commissions, as well as departments of water or power, are proprietary agencies that control their own budgets. They are therefore somewhat independent of both the council and mayor even though they are appointed by the mayor.

INTERGOVERNMENTAL COOPERATION

Cities do not stand alone. They have responsibilities to, and are affected by, the actions of other levels of government, and work in cooperation with them on issues of concern to city residents.

City-County Connections

Cities and counties have very strong ties. Cities benefit from county assessment rolls and county tax collection services. A county may provide money for city street construction that benefits the county's road system. The two jurisdictions often cooperate in building and operating parks, libraries, and other public facilities. City and county fire and law enforcement officers work together under mutual aid agreements, usually established for emergency situations.

The state Legislature can require counties to perform specified services at the request of the cities within them. Most cities that request these services are small communities.

The Joint Exercise of Powers Act (passed in 2000) allows any two or more public agencies that share a common power to formally agree to jointly implement programs, build facilities, or deliver services. Officials create JPAs to cut costs, be more efficient, reduce overlapping services, and share resources.

What does that mean?

JPA is an acronym used for three different terms:
- Joint Powers Agreement
- Joint Powers Agency
- Joint Powers Authority

California law permits the creation of Joint Powers Authorities and they are widely used throughout the state. A Joint Powers Authority permits two or more public agencies or authorities, like local governments, transit districts or other special districts, to operate collectively or jointly, but limits them to their combined territorial jurisdictions. Joint Powers Authorities receive power from the creating agencies or governments, unlike special districts which receive their power directly from the state.

Current examples of Joint Powers Authorities include the Transbay JPA, a collective of transportation boards and counties around the San Francisco Bay area created to promote the construction of a new transit center; the Southern California Public Power Authority, which has 12 public power agency members; and the California Fire and Rescue Training Authority, which is comprised of three agencies: Office of Emergency Services—Fire and Rescue Branch, the Sacramento Fire Department, and the Sacramento Metropolitan Fire District. For more information: <fireandrescuetraining.ca.gov/cfrta-member-agencies.aspx>.

For more information, see *"Governments Working Together: A Citizen's Guide to Joint Powers Agreements"* and <senweb03.senate.ca.gov/committee/standing/GOVERNANCE/GWTFinalversion2.pdf>.

City-State Connections

All California residents, whether living in unincorporated areas or in cities, are subject to state law. City police enforce state laws along with municipal ordinances.

While city governments may affect local or municipal affairs, there are important limitations on their power to do so. Passage of local legislation must avoid conflicts with state law; if any conflict occurs, the state law is the one enforced. Local ordinances may not authorize acts prohibited by state statute or prohibit acts specifically authorized by the Legislature.

Local ordinances are not applicable to state agencies unless the state consents – for example, the state consents to administer local sales taxes.

State power overrides local power when the state is deemed to have broader authority in the field. For instance, by adopting the California Vehicle Code, the Legislature has prevented cities from enacting their own traffic regulations except as expressly authorized in the state code. Cities are also preempted in narcotics law and alcoholic beverage control, with no exceptions. In many decisions, the courts have invalidated local regulations based on a finding that the Legislature had the intent to preempt the area in question.

The state also sets standards in areas affecting public health, safety, welfare, and the environment. Although cities are allowed to exceed state standards, when a minimum standard is set by the state it is applicable to all cities. Exceptions are allowed in some instances – for example, in state building code requirements – if they are found necessary because of local conditions.

Cities receive very little of their money (less than 10 percent) from the state. Because Proposition 13 sharply limits property taxes, cities have often used special taxes, fees and charges to raise money for local services, but several state initiatives have limited their ability to do this. Many special taxes must be expended for state or local purposes as specified by the

Legislature. For instance, gas tax funds must be used for construction and maintenance of city streets or for mass transit. Vehicle fines must be spent for traffic control and traffic law enforcement.

A city may contract with the state or county for personnel services. Employees of many cities participate in the state system of retirement benefits.

City-Federal Connections

The federal government has little direct control over cities; nevertheless, money from federal agencies may be channeled through county or state agencies and reach local governments in the form of grants. Cities also benefit from direct federal grants and loans for community facilities and mass transportation, and from federal funding of housing agencies. Some federal control over cities is exerted through the criteria established for federal funding. Through these requirements the federal government may promote nondiscriminatory housing, environmental improvement, and citizen participation in governmental decision-making.

Special Districts

In California, many local government functions are carried out through a system of special districts – a concept that was invented and developed in this state. A special district is a separate local government unit that delivers a specified number of public services to a geographically limited area. California uses the special district form of local government on a wider scale than any other state in the nation.

The size of the area served by a special district can vary tremendously. A lighting district, for instance, can be as small as one square block, while some water districts encompass several counties. Special districts deliver many different kinds of services, not only water and electricity, but also mosquito abatement, irrigation, and fire protection. Most special districts serve just a single purpose, such as sewage treatment. Others respond to a wide range of needs, as in the case of community service districts, which can deliver up to 32 services. Special districts have distinctive characteristics: They all

Find special districts on a map: <csda.net/component/content/article/2113>.

- are a specific form of local government

- have governing boards
- provide services and facilities
- have defined boundaries.

Special districts have many of the same powers as counties and cities. They can sign contracts, employ workers, and acquire real property through purchase or eminent domain. They can also issue bonds, impose special taxes, levy benefit assessments, and charge service fees. Like other governments, special districts can sue and be sued; however, only rarely do they have police powers.

Special districts are not school districts, which are established to provide only one service – education. School districts receive much of their money from the state, but special districts are funded locally.

 The California Special District Association <csda.net/> provides training for its members and facilitates the exchange of news and information.

Single-Purpose/Multipurpose Activities

Most special districts perform a single function such as street lighting or fire protection. About 10 percent of special districts serve more than one function and are called multipurpose districts. In unincorporated areas, county service areas are often used to provide a variety of services to rural areas and small communities that do not have a large enough tax base to pay for them individually (<californiataxdata.com/pdf/CountyServiceArea.pdf>). The state also makes it possible for unincorporated areas to initiate the formation of a community service district to provide local services (<californiataxdata.com/pdf/CSD.pdf>). These are examples of multipurpose special districts.

Enterprise/Non-Enterprise Activities

Enterprise activities are financed entirely or predominantly by user fees set at a level to cover costs.

Non-enterprise activities are supported primarily by general revenue sources such as taxes.

Just over a quarter of the special districts are enterprise districts. Enterprise districts deliver services that are run like business enterprises – they charge for their customers' services. For example, a hospital district charges room fees paid by the patient's insurance, not by the district's other residents. Water districts charge water rates to their customers. Nearly all of the water, wastewater, and hospital districts are enterprise districts.

Non-enterprise districts provide services which don't lend themselves to fees. Fire protection services and mosquito abatement programs benefit the entire community, not just individual residents. No direct cost/benefit relationship exists in the services provided by non-enterprise districts. Consequently, non-enterprise districts generally don't charge user fees for their services. No one wants to put a meter on a park district's swings or charge residents to put out a house fire. Non-enterprise districts rely overwhelmingly on property tax revenues and parcel taxes to pay their operational expenses. Services commonly provided by non-enterprise districts include cemeteries, fire protection, libraries, and police protection. Although non-enterprise districts rely primarily on non-fee revenue, certain services, such as a recreation and park district's swimming pool or soccer programs, can generate some fee revenue.*

> * *What's So Special About Special Districts?*
> *(Fourth Edition).* Sacramento CA: California
> Legislature, Senate Local Government Committee,
> October 2010.

See Figure 9.1, on the next page, for the various sources of revenue for special districts.

Independent and Dependent Districts

An independent district operates under a locally elected, independent board of directors, while a dependent district operates under the control of a county board of supervisors or

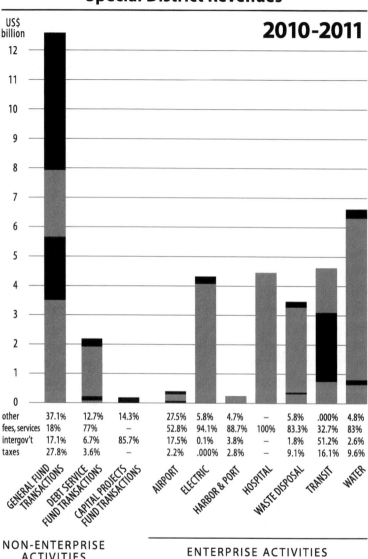

Figure 9.1   **Special District Revenues**

2010-2011

US$ billion

	GENERAL FUND TRANSACTIONS	DEBT SERVICE FUND TRANSACTIONS	CAPITAL PROJECTS FUND TRANSACTIONS	AIRPORT	ELECTRIC	HARBOR & PORT	HOSPITAL	WASTE DISPOSAL	TRANSIT	WATER
other	37.1%	12.7%	14.3%	27.5%	5.8%	4.7%	–	5.8%	.000%	4.8%
fees, services	18%	77%	–	52.8%	94.1%	88.7%	100%	83.3%	32.7%	83%
intergov't	17.1%	6.7%	85.7%	17.5%	0.1%	3.8%	–	1.8%	51.2%	2.6%
taxes	27.8%	3.6%	–	2.2%	.000%	2.8%	–	9.1%	16.1%	9.6%

NON-ENTERPRISE ACTIVITIES
supported primarily by general revenue sources such as taxes

ENTERPRISE ACTIVITIES
financed entirely or predominantly by user fees set at a level to cover costs

data from the Office of the State Controller:
<sco.ca.gov/Files-ARD-Local/LocRep/2010-11_Special_District.pdf>

a city council. About two-thirds of the state's special districts are independent districts. The registered voters in a county usually elect the special district's board of directors, although in some water districts only landowners are allowed to vote.

If You'd Like to Learn More ...

Like hula hoops, martinis, and freeways, special districts became an art form in California. Special districts first arose to meet the water needs of San Joaquin Valley farmers. Frustrated by an inconsistent water supply and unstable prices, farmers in Stanislaus County organized the Turlock Irrigation District under the Wright Act of 1887. The Wright Act allowed landowners to form new public entities to deliver irrigation water, and to finance their activities with water rates and bond sales. As California's first special district, the Turlock Irrigation District made it possible for local farmers to intensify and diversify their crops.

While the earliest irrigation districts served rural areas, the trend was toward delivering water to urban and suburban communities. In the early 1900s, water districts were primarily located in northern and central California. After 1950, they spread to southern California to satisfy the growing suburban water demands.

In the 20th century, special districts increased dramatically in both number and scope. The periods of prosperity and population growth that followed both world wars increased the demand for public services of all kinds and, consequently, special districts. Special districts became a popular way to meet these needs. Unlike the complex bureaucracies that can come with cityhood, special districts were flexible and provided desired services quickly and efficiently.

The statutory authorization for mosquito abatement districts in 1915 shows the recurring connection between the real estate industry and the desire for local services. Salt marsh mosquitoes around the San Francisco Bay and higher than average malaria cases in rural counties prompted legislators to allow local officials to form mosquito abatement districts. The 372 fire protection districts can trace their origins to a 1923 state law. In 1931, the Legislature authorized recreation districts, the forerunners of today's 108 recreation and park districts. Hospital districts arose in 1945 because of a statewide shortage of hospital beds. Although originally created to address individual services, special districts later encompassed multiple needs. The Legislature provided for multipurpose county service areas in 1953 and community services districts in 1961.*

What's So Special About Special Districts? (Fourth Edition) Senate Local Government Committee, October 2010.

Formation and Change of Special Districts

Some counties encourage unincorporated communities to form independent districts when services are needed, so that local responsibility is maximized. Other counties prefer the formation of dependent districts, so that provision of services remains more firmly under county policy direction. Still other counties discourage the formation of special districts altogether, preferring that an area either annex itself to a city or form a new city to obtain needed services.

No special district may be formed without authorization by the state. The state Legislature has authorized 55 general types of district formation and operation. Each type has its own unique subset of features in terms of the number and type of activities authorized, funding and taxing authority, and governing body.

Role of the Local Agency Formation Commission
(LAFCo)

Every county has a Local Agency Formation Commission. The LAFCo generally has five members: two county supervisors, two city council members, and one at-large or public member. Some LAFCos add two representatives from independent special districts, for a total of seven members.

Formed by the Legislature in 1963 to apply state policies and regulations, LAFCos are legally independent of county, city, and special district governments. The Legislature established a LAFCo in each county in an effort to discourage urban sprawl and ensure orderly formation and development of local governments.

Each LAFCo has two main responsibilities:

1. To determine the sphere of influence for each city and special district within the county. The sphere of influence is the area into which each local agency can extend its services. This information helps a commission decide which configuration and type of agency is best suited to provide public services to a particular area.

2. To review and act on requests to form or dissolve a local agency or to change the organization or boundaries of an existing agency. LAFCo considers the impact the proposal might have on the environment, on the residents of nearby areas, on other local agencies, and on the distribution of property tax. The commission can then take one of three actions: it can reject the proposal, approve it outright, or approve it subject to certain conditions or modifications.

Board of Supervisors' Role

Upon approval by LAFCo, a proposal to form or change a local government's boundaries or structure is sent to the county board of supervisors. The supervisors hold a public hearing and review any protests received. If there are no protests from a majority of the area's voters, the board places the issue on the ballot. Majority voter approval is required.

Paying for Government

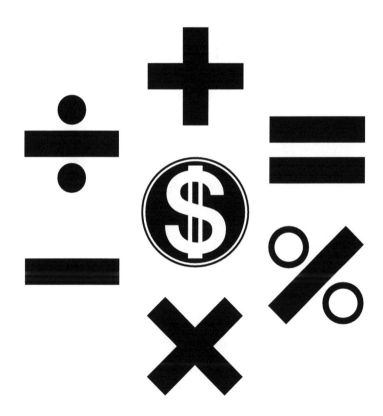

PART IV

Budget and Finance

Californians tell their representatives what they want their government to do, but that leaves officials with the huge task of setting up a budget and funding all the mandated activities. Each level of government in California operates within a budget, which contains an estimate of available funds and revenues and a spending plan for a particular year. Nearly all levels of government consider July 1 the beginning of a budget or fiscal year and June 30 as the end of the fiscal year

---

What does that mean?

Revenue: the income of a government from taxation, excise duties, customs, or other sources

Fiscal: of or relating to public revenues (taxation), public spending, debt, and other financial matters

---

OVERVIEW OF GOVERNMENT BUDGETS

The California Constitution requires that the governor submit a budget to the Legislature by January 10. If the proposed expenditures for the budget year exceed estimated revenues, the governor is required to recommend the sources for additional funding. The federal government is much freer to borrow money; federal officials may deliberately plan to spend more than they expect to take in. The federal government is permitted to incur heavy, long-term debt in its efforts to influence the economy. At the state level, the governor must present a balanced budget proposal. In order to borrow money against the General Fund by issuing bonds, the Legislature must pass, and the governor must sign, a bill to put the proposal before the voters.

Governments get their money from taxes, fees, sales of bonds and from other levels of government. Very often the source of these revenues controls their use. For example, most of the money collected from motor vehicle taxes must be spent for transportation purposes. When the state gives money to the counties or cities, it usually restricts the ways in which that money can be spent.

The funds from various revenue sources are separated into several categories:

1. Money for a specific purpose is placed in a special revenue fund.
2. The proceeds from each bond issued for a capital improvement go into a capital project fund.
3. Revenues from self-supporting government operations are held in enterprise funds.
4. All revenues not earmarked for a specific purpose go into the General Fund.

Budgeting in any government is, to a great extent, automatic and mechanical. Although California has used concepts such as Zero-Based Budgeting (ZBB), Management By Objectives

Cal Facts: a broad overview of public finance and program trends in California from the LAO, the Legislative Analyst's Office (the legislature's nonpartisan fiscal and policy advisor). <lao.ca.gov/>.

44 states require the governor to propose a balanced budget: http://www. nasbo.org/ sites/default/ files/2015%20 Budget%20 Processes%20 -%20S.pdf, page 52. (60 of 162 in PDF).

(MBO), and Total Quality Management (TQM), the basic approach utilized now is incremental budgeting. This approach uses the current level of funding for a department as a base amount to be adjusted by change proposals. Many obligations, such as for debt service, are legally required; others such as retirement and other fringe benefits secured by union contracts must be paid, along with utility costs. The effects of inflation require cost-of-living adjustments (COLAs) merely to maintain the same levels of services. However, COLAs are governed by statute and thus are subject to change. In recent years, automatic COLAs in a number of programs have been eliminated.

The NASBO report lists 41 states requiring the legislature to pass a balanced budget.

Because so much government spending is required by law, only part of the General Fund is actually available for discretionary spending. This discretionary portion is the focus of most of the debate during the budget process. The Budget Change Proposal (BCP) has been the traditional decision document which proposes a change to the existing budget level. The BCPs are submitted by departments to the Department of Finance for review and analysis.

State Budget Process
Both the administrative and the legislative branches of government have roles in the process leading to the adoption of the budget. In California this process takes a full fourteen months. In May and June, planning is underway for the fiscal year that will begin July 1 of the next calendar year.

Governor's Proposal

1. During the spring, each department reviews expenditure plans and prepares a baseline budget to maintain services. They may also prepare BCPs to change levels of service. These are submitted to the Department of Finance for review.
2. The Department of Finance prepares a balanced expenditure plan for the governor's approval.

Find the Department of Finance's summary of the governor's annual budget <dof.ca.gov/budget/>.

3. The governor's budget is released to the Legislature by January 10th of each year. Two identical budget bills are prepared: one for the Assembly and one for the Senate.
4. The governor issues a State of the State address setting forth policy goals for the coming fiscal year. Two identical budget bills are prepared: one for the Assembly and one for the Senate.

The Legislature and the Budget

1. In the Assembly, the budget bill is introduced by the chair of the Budget Committee, and in the Senate by the chair of the Budget and Fiscal Review Committee.
2. The Legislative Analyst's Office analyzes the governor's proposed budget and publishes a series of reports on overarching fiscal issues, major new proposals, and specific departmental programs, along with its recommendations for legislative action.

3. The budget committee of each house is divided into budget subcommittees which conduct public hearings on assigned sections of the budget, usually in March, April, and May. Any private citizen, interest group, legislative advocate, or government staff member may address a budget subcommittee to advocate a higher or lower spending level for a particular program. The decisions of the budget subcommittees are significant. Traditionally, the full committees accept the subcommittee recommendations with little or no alteration; only a few items are debated and changed by the full committees.
4. By this process each house develops its own revised version of the budget bill, triggering the need for a conference committee.
5. The Budget Conference Committee consists of three Senate and three Assembly members. Responsibility

for chairing the conference committee alternates annually between both houses. The conference committee holds public hearings during June and attempts to resolve the policy and fiscal differences between the Assembly and Senate versions of the budget. On issues where the conference committee is unable to work out the differences between the two versions of the budget, the legislative leadership and the governor meet privately to reach a compromise.

Prop 25, passed by the voters in 2010, reduces the number of votes required to pass the budget and related trailer bills in the Legislature from two-thirds (⅔) to a majority.

6. The agreed-upon budget bill is sent by the Budget Conference Committee to the floor of each house. Both houses must approve the compromise budget by a simple majority vote. A simple majority vote is also required to pass the "trailer bills" that make any statutory changes needed to implement provisions of the budget bill.

7. The final budget package is submitted to the governor for signature.

If you want to know more ...

The legislative analyst plays a key role in the budget process as the Legislature's main financial adviser. The LAO publishes an Overview of the Governor's Budget with its initial response to the budget proposal and follows it with a number of publications that discuss selected programs in more detail, including background information and evaluation of the budget request, and the analyst's recommendations for future spending. The analyst's recommendation may differ considerably from the governor's proposals. A program which is criticized by the legislative analyst sometimes turns into a controversial budget program.

Find the legislative analyst's overview and analysis of budget issues at <lao.ca.gov/>.

The legislative analyst can also suggest that certain portions of the tax structure be carefully scrutinized. The analyst's recommendation may be to change a particular tax rate or to modify or eliminate certain tax exemptions, deductions, exclusions, or credits, since each such exception to a general tax rule represents lost revenue.

The LAO also analyzes the updated estimates of program needs and revenues issued in May by the Department of Finance. Other legislative analyst publications include a report on the budget as enacted and an annual Fiscal Outlook that looks at possible state revenue and spending trends over the next five years.

See Figure 10.1 The Annual Budget Process

Adoption of the Budget

When the budget bill receives a simple majority vote of each house, it is passed on to the governor. The state Constitution allows the governor to reduce or eliminate an item of appropriation.

The Constitution prohibits the Legislature from sending to the governor, and the governor from signing, a budget bill that would appropriate from the General Fund a total amount that exceeds General Fund revenue. In other words the budget must be balanced.

When the Budget Act has been signed, the Department of Finance publishes, on its website, the final budget summary and details of changes between the January 10 budget and the enacted budget. <dof.ca.gov/>.

State Income Overview

California derives its income from its own taxes and fees, from the federal government, and from the sale of bonds. About three-quarters of the proceeds from taxes and fees imposed by the state go into the General Fund. The others are special fund revenues. The three largest General Fund revenue sources are the personal income tax, the sales and use tax, and the corporation tax.

Figure 10.1   # The Annual Budget Process

EXECUTIVE DEPARTMENTS
review expenditure plans
annually prepare baseline budgets to maintain existing levels of services
may prepare Budget Change Proposals (BCPs) to change levels of service

DEPARTMENT OF FINANCE
analyzes the baseline budget and BCPs, focusing on the fiscal impact

---

GOVERNOR   **submits proposed budget in January**

LEGISLATURE   budget bill introduced

Legislative Analyst's Office (LAO)
prepares analysis and overview

PUBLIC input
to the governor,
members of the
Legislature and
subcommittees

SENATE BUDGET AND FISCAL REVIEW COMMITTEE	**ASSEMBLY BUDGET COMMITTEE**
▮▮▮▮	▮▮▮▮
SUBCOMMITTEES	**SUBCOMMITTEES**
▮▮▮▮	▮▮▮▮

GOVERNOR   submits the "May Revision"

▮▮▮▮   ▮▮▮▮
Senate Budget Bill   Assembly Budget Bill

BUDGET CONFERENCE COMMITTEE   reconciles with both the Legislature and the governor, adopts a budget

LEGISLATURE   votes on budget

� *simple majority vote required for passage* ▬▬▬

GOVERNOR   **signs budget**

INDIVIDUAL DEPARTMENTS AND THE DEPARTMENT OF FINANCE
continually administer, manage change, exercise oversight of the budget

the Joint Legislative Budget Committee (JLBC) provides some coordination between the two houses and oversees the LAO

the JLBC is involved in the ongoing administration of the budget and reviews various requests for changes to the budget, after enactment

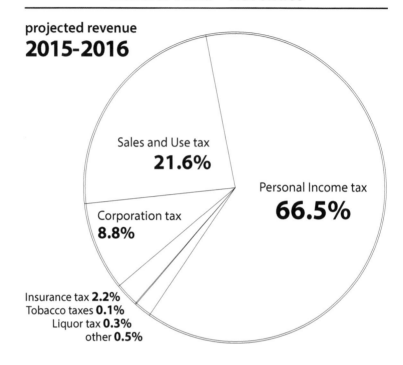

Figure 10.2 **General Fund – Revenues**

projected revenue
2015-2016

Sales and Use tax
21.6%

Personal Income tax
66.5%

Corporation tax
8.8%

Insurance tax **2.2%**
Tobacco taxes **0.1%**
Liquor tax **0.3%**
other **0.5%**

General Fund

The state budget focuses on the General Fund, which raises its money from several major tax sources. Figure 10.2 shows the percentages coming from each source for fiscal year 2015–16.

Changing Sources of Tax Funding

The personal income tax was implemented in 1935 and is the single largest General Fund revenue source (66 percent). The tax is on personal income and the tax rate brackets, standard deduction, and personal and dependent credits are based on the June California Consumer Price Index. This tax is administered by the Franchise Tax Board.

The sales and use tax was implemented in 1933 and is the

Figure 10.3 **General Fund – Changing Proportions**

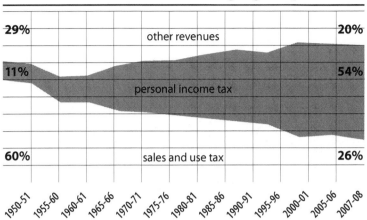

second single largest General Fund revenue source (22 percent). The state government and local governments share this tax. Currently, the state's rate is 6 percent while local rates may vary from 1.5 percent to 4.0 percent. The tax is imposed on sales of tangible property, but there are numerous exclusions, including food for home consumption, prescription medications, and a variety of other goods ranging from custom computer programs to aircraft. This tax is administered by the Board of Equalization.

The bank and corporation tax was implemented in 1929 and is the third largest General Fund revenue (9 percent). The tax is imposed on corporate income attributable to California activities. This tax is administered by the Franchise Tax Board.

The insurance gross premiums tax, cigarette tax, alcoholic beverage tax, and various licenses and fees account for about 3 percent of General Fund revenues.

Special Funds
The California Constitution and state statutes specify into

which funds certain revenues must be deposited and how they are to be spent. These revenues are accounted for in various special funds. In general, special fund revenues include three categories of income:

- receipts from tax levies, which are allocated to specified functions, such as motor vehicle taxes and fees
- charges such as business and professional license fees
- rental royalties and other receipts designated for a particular purpose, such as oil and gas royalties

Total special fund revenues are estimated to be $45.7 billion in 2015–16. About 25 percent of all special fund revenue in 2015–16 is expected to come from taxes and fees related to motor vehicles. The principal sources are motor vehicle fees (registration, weight, and vehicle license fees) and motor vehicle fuel taxes. During 2015–16, it is expected that about $11.4 billion in revenues will be derived from the ownership or operation of motor vehicles. Over one-third of motor vehicle fuel tax revenues will be allocated to local governments for local road projects, and the remaining portion will be used for state transportation programs.

Federal Funds

The money that comes to the state treasury from the federal government is placed into special accounts. The federal dollars are then redistributed to programs and individuals as required by federal laws and regulations.

The amount of federal aid received by California has been and continues to be very volatile. Debates in Washington about the federal government's debt limits and spending affect every state. California depends on federal funding for research in higher education, special education funding, plans for high-speed rail development, and many other projects. It is impossible to predict how federal funding trends will affect California in coming years.

Figure 10.4 **General Fund Revenue Volatility**

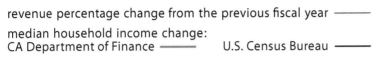

revenue percentage change from the previous fiscal year ———

median household income change:
CA Department of Finance ——————   U.S. Census Bureau ———

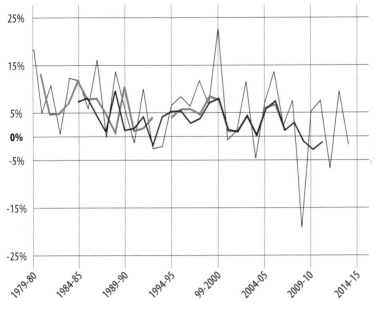

CA DOF notes: data for 1994 onward are not comparable to prior historical data because of the current population survey redesign

Bonds

Each year the state budget anticipates receiving money from the sale of bonds; the amount expected varies depending on the number of bonds that have been authorized for sale and their attractiveness to investors. The state bond program is the most effective way for the state to borrow large sums of money. State bonds are used to purchase, build, or develop major facilities such as parklands and school facilities. Further information about bonds can be found on the state treasurer's website <treasurer.ca.gov/>.

Types of Bonds

A bond is an interest-bearing certificate issued by the government as a promise to repay a loan to the government at the end of a specified period, usually 20 or 30 years. The purchaser of the bond is lending money to the government. The government periodically pays bond purchasers a specified interest rate. The holder of the bond does not have to pay income tax on the interest received. There are several types of bonds issued:

1. **Revenue Bond**. A bond repaid using money earned by the project which was financed by that bond. For example, rent received for college dormitory rooms goes toward the repayment of the bond sold to build the dorms. There is no ceiling on the interest rate that the government may offer the lender. State revenue bonds must be authorized by a majority vote of both houses of the Legislature. Voter authorization is not required.

2. **General Obligation Bond**. A bond repaid using money from the General Fund. State general obligation bonds must be authorized by a two-thirds vote of both houses of the Legislature and a majority vote of the people, and their repayment is guaranteed by the state's general taxing powers. Counties, cities, and special districts are also authorized to issue general obligation bonds.

3. **Lease Revenue Bond**. Typically used to finance a state facility such as a prison or state office building, this bond is paid off from lease payments by the state agency using the facility, primarily through General Fund appropriations. Lease-revenue bonds must be authorized by a majority vote of both houses of the Legislature, but voter authorization is not required.

4. **Special Assessment Bond**. Sold by counties, cities and special districts to finance public works projects like streets and sewers. Each landowner in the area served by the capital improvement pays an amount based on the share of the benefit received by that parcel of

property.

Bond Rating.

A government bond is rated by a rating agency at the time of sale as to its soundness as an investment. The rating on a general obligation bond depends on the ability of the state to raise sufficient revenues to assure regular payments to the purchaser of the bond. The lower the rating, the higher the interest the government must pay.

Over the years California's credit rating has generally been high, but during the past decade it has declined and is now improving somewhat. The rankings given by three of the most widely-used financial rating services are shown in Figure 10.5.

Property Taxes

Terms You Should Know:

Real property: Land and improvements that are permanently attached, such as buildings and houses, including mobile homes located on permanent foundations. Most real property is subject to the property tax. Real property owned by a church, governmental entity, or bank is exempt from the property tax.

Personal property: Movable, unsecured property. Includes business furnishings and equipment, boats, aircraft, and railroad cars. Excludes home furnishings and business inventories.

Full cash value (market value): The highest amount a willing and knowledgeable seller of property could obtain from a willing and knowledgeable buyer.

Assessed value: Under Proposition 13, set at full cash value as of 1975-76 with growth in the assessed value restricted to a 2 percent annual increase. Real property is only reassessed to reflect full cash value of new construction or the full cash value at the time of the sale or change of ownership. About 18 percent of all properties statewide change hands in a given year and thus are reassessed to current value.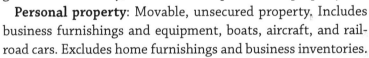

Tax rate: Limited by Proposition 13 to 1 percent of assessed value. The tax rate cannot exceed $1 per $100 of assessed valuation plus whatever additional rate is needed to cover voter-approved debt, such as bonds. The overall rate varies somewhat across the state, but is generally about 1.1 percent.

Board of Equalization: Responsible for standardizing assessment practices within and among California's counties. Grants property tax exemptions for property dedicated to health, educational, and charitable purposes.

Historical Background of Property Taxes in California

Prior to 1912, the state derived up to 70 percent of its revenue from property taxes. The state no longer relies on property taxes as its primary source of funds. Since 1933, the only property tax directly levied, collected, and retained by the state has been the tax on privately owned railroad cars. Currently, the state's principal revenue sources are personal income taxes, sales and use taxes, bank and corporation taxes, and a series of excise taxes. The State Board of Equalization (BOE) administers sales and use taxes and excise taxes, while the Franchise Tax Board administers the personal income and bank and corporation taxes. Today, it is California's counties, cities, schools, and special districts that depend on the property tax as a primary source of revenue. The property tax raised more than $52.2 billion for local government during 2013–14. These funds were allocated as follows: counties 15 percent, cities 12 percent, schools (school districts and community colleges) 54 percent, and special districts 19 percent.

Proposition 13. On June 6, 1978, California voters overwhelmingly approved Proposition 13, a property tax limitation initiative. This amendment to California's Constitution was the taxpayers' collective response to dramatic increases in property taxes and a growing state revenue surplus of nearly $5 billion. Proposition 13 rolled back most local real property, or real estate, assessments to 1975 market value levels, limited the property tax rate to 1 percent plus the rate necessary to

Figure 10.5 ## CA Credit Rating History

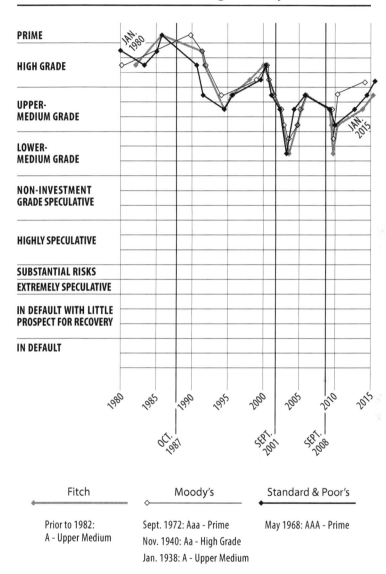

PRIME

HIGH GRADE

UPPER-
MEDIUM GRADE

LOWER-
MEDIUM GRADE

NON-INVESTMENT
GRADE SPECULATIVE

HIGHLY SPECULATIVE

SUBSTANTIAL RISKS
EXTREMELY SPECULATIVE

IN DEFAULT WITH LITTLE
PROSPECT FOR RECOVERY

IN DEFAULT

Fitch	Moody's	Standard & Poor's
Prior to 1982:	Sept. 1972: Aaa - Prime	May 1968: AAA - Prime
A - Upper Medium	Nov. 1940: Aa - High Grade	
	Jan. 1938: A - Upper Medium	

data courtesy of California State Treasurer: <treasurer.ca.gov/ratings/history.asp>

fund local voter-approved bonded indebtedness, and limited future property tax increases.

After Proposition 13, county property tax revenues dropped from $10.3 billion in 1977–78 to $5.04 billion in 1978–79. As a result, many local governments were in fiscal crisis. Keeping local governments in operation the first two years following Proposition 13 required legislative "bailouts" to offset property tax revenue losses. A first-year stopgap measure costing $4.17 billion in state surplus funds was necessary to directly aid local governments. A second-year bailout, a long-term fiscal relief plan, cost the state $4.85 billion.

Prior to 1978, real property was appraised cyclically, with no more than a five-year interval between reassessments. This kept assessed values at or near current market value levels. In contrast, under Proposition 13, properties are reassessed to current market value only upon a change in ownership or completion of new construction (called the base year value). In addition, Proposition 13 generally limits annual increases in the base year value of real property to no more than 2 percent, except when property changes ownership or undergoes new construction. Essentially, Proposition 13 converted the market value-based property tax system to an acquisition value-based system.

Disparities in Assessed Value. Under Proposition 13, similar properties can have substantially different assessed values based on the dates the properties were purchased. Disparities result wherever significant appreciation in property values has occurred over time. Longtime property owners, whose assessed values generally may not be increased more than 2 percent per year, tend to have lower tax liability than recent purchasers, whose assessed values tend to approximate market levels.

Court Challenges to Proposition 13. Immediately after Proposition 13 passed, its constitutionality was challenged.

The California Supreme Court upheld the constitutionality of Proposition 13 in *Amador Valley Joint Union High School District v. State Board of Equalization* on September 22, 1978. The decision rendered in this case remained the highest judicial ruling on Proposition 13 until 1992, when the United States Supreme Court ruled, in *Nordlinger v. Hahn,* that Proposition 13 did not violate the equal protection clause of the United States Constitution. This ruling effectively ended speculation about whether the judicial system would ever overturn or modify Proposition 13.*

> *Information taken from the Board of Equalization publication 29: California Property Tax: an Overview (2015) <boe.ca.gov/proptaxes/pdf/pub29.pdf>.

LOCAL GOVERNMENT BUDGETS

Local government units include counties, cities, special districts, and school and community college districts. Their budgets are matters of public record and are subject to public hearings before adoption by the governing boards.

State and federal funds, passed down to local governments for disbursement, provide a great portion of their income. For additional money to provide services, local governments have traditionally relied heavily on the property tax, the oldest form of taxation. Since the passage of Proposition 13 in 1978, local governments have relied less on property taxes and more on service fees and other taxes. In 2004 and 2010, respectively, Propositions 1A and 22 were enacted to protect local revenues from state reallocation.

In recent years funding for local governments has changed frequently because of changes in legislation and state funding.

Government websites are the most reliable sources for current information on finance because print sources become outdated very quickly. The State and Local Government on the Net website <statelocalgov.net/state-ca.cfm> offers a list of websites for counties and other government units.

Financing Counties

General revenues for counties come from a variety of sources. State and federal government provide nearly half of the total; the counties must spend these funds for specific purposes, primarily health and social service programs. Other significant county revenue sources are property taxes (19 percent of county revenues in 2012-13) and user charges and enterprise revenues (22 percent in 2012-013).

Financing Cities

Charter cities are authorized by the California Constitution to impose any tax not specifically prohibited by the state. General law cities may levy only those taxes expressly permitted by the Legislature. However, the Legislature has extended the taxing authority held by charter cities to general law cities.

Local governments set taxes taxes (where not otherwise restricted by state law) and fees so that city councils can vary the rates of business licenses, hotel taxes, charges for municipal services, and fees for development permits. Cities have greater flexibility than counties in their ability to produce revenue. Cities have access to about 20 kinds of tax and non-tax funds from local, state, and federal sources.

Comparing revenues and expenditures of different cities can be difficult because they vary according to the needs of residents and the responsibilities of the city. Less than 25 percent of cities are full-service cities responsible for all services, including fire service, library, police, parks and others. The majority of cities have special districts to pay for one or more of these services.

Figure 10.6   **Typical CA City Revenues**

Cities receive a significant share of their funding from various user charges. Cities use these funds to pay for electric, water, and other municipal services. Over one-third of city revenues come from local taxes, the largest of which is the property tax.

2012-2013

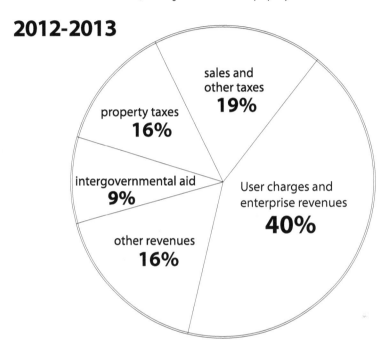

data courtesy Legislative Analyst's Office:
www.lao.ca.gov/reports/2014/calfacts/calfacts-2014.aspx

Figure 10.6 Typical CA City Revenues was prepared by The League of California Cities <cacities.org/>.

Financing Special Districts

Special districts rely primarily on three local revenue sources: user charges or service fees, property taxes, and special assessments. The level of dependence on one or more of them varies according to the kind of district and type of service provided. Enterprise activities such as water supply and sewage disposal are supported entirely by user charges or service fees.

In contrast, non-enterprise special districts, such as fire protection and parks and recreation districts, rely heavily on property taxes for revenues. Non-enterprise districts have also turned to operating a greater number of programs and services on a self-supporting basis, charging the individual user a fee high enough to pay for the full cost the program, rather than subsidizing the service with general tax dollars.

In addition, with few exceptions, special districts are authorized to borrow money for major construction projects by issuing bonds, subject to voter approval.

Providing Public Education

PART V

The Educational System CHAPTER 11

Public education plays a role in the lives of almost all Californians. More than 90 percent of the state's students attend public schools for their elementary and high school education. Voters demonstrate their support of education by approving ballot initiatives that benefit schools, colleges, and universities.

Portsmouth Plaza, San Francisco, was the site of the first public school in California in 1848.

The U.S. Constitution has made public education the responsibility of each state. Thus the nation has 50 state school systems differing widely in organization, financial resources, and effectiveness. The public school system in California is the largest in the nation, serving more than 6.2 million students in 2013-14. California law requires everyone between the ages of six and eighteen to attend school, except sixteen- and seventeen-year-olds who have graduated from high school or passed the California High School Proficiency Exam (CHSPE) and obtained parental permission to leave. Adult education programs, community colleges, the California State University system, and the University of California system offer opportunities for lifelong learning.

If you want more background ...

The laws governing education in the state are contained in the *California Education Code*. The full text is available online at the California Legislative Information site <leginfo.legislature.ca.gov/faces/codes. xhtml>.

ELEMENTARY AND SECONDARY EDUCATION

The number of pupils in grades K–12 is expected to grow 1.1% by 2021.

The state government shares responsibility for California's public schools with local school districts. The Legislature requires the formation of local districts and grants certain powers to them. State laws require specific programs and courses of study and provide a growing percentage of school funding.

DEPARTMENT OF EDUCATION

The **California superintendent of public instruction**, a constitutional officer elected without party affiliation to a four-year term, directs the Department of Education. The superintendent is the chief administrative officer of the public school system and provides leadership in developing and implementing strategies to improve education in the state's public schools. The superintendent also serves as an ex officio member of the governing boards of the University of California and the California State University.

The **State Board of Education** (SBE) is the governing and policymaking body of the California Department of Education. The SBE sets K-12 (kindergarten through twelfth grade) education policy in the areas of standards, instructional materials, assessment, and accountability. The SBE adopts textbooks for grades K-8, adopts regulations to implement legislation, and has authority to grant waivers of the Education Code. The SBE has 11 members, appointed by the governor, who serve without pay. The superintendent of public instruction serves as secretary and executive officer of the board. While the board develops general policy, both the Legislature and local school boards exert strong influence on educational policies and programs.

California has 10,366 grade K–12 public schools with 6.2 million students. These schools have 581,179 FTE (full-time-equivalent) staff members.

The **Department of Education** develops and administers programs which are implemented by local school districts. Although many of these programs are incorporated into regular classroom instruction, others require special facilities and considerable supervision at the state level.

The department administers a variety of childcare and developmental programs that provide a full or part-day comprehensive program for young children. These subsidized services are provided to low-income families while parents are going to school, participating in training programs, working, or seeking employment.

If you want more background ...

The department oversees services to students with disabilities who require special services. In 2011, the California Legislature passed Assembly Bill 114, which repealed the 1984 requirement that school districts form partnerships with county mental health agencies to provide mental health services to students with individualized education programs. As a result of this new legislation, school districts are solely responsible for ensuring that students with disabilities receive special education and related services to meet their needs according to the federal Individuals with Disabilities Education Act (IDEA) of 2004. For further information about the "guidance documents" concerning the provision of related special education services, see this chart <cde.ca.gov/sp/se/ac/documents/guidancedocrltdsrvc.pdf >.

The Department of Education operates three residential schools and three diagnostic centers to serve the unique needs of special education students. The California School for the Blind in Fremont and the California School for the Deaf campuses in Riverside and Fremont provide comprehensive education and related services to the state's visually impaired and aurally impaired students. The diagnostic centers, located in San Francisco, Fresno, and Los Angeles, provide assessment services for special education students throughout California. Additionally, the centers provide support services to local education agencies, service organizations, and other education-related groups.

COUNTY OFFICES OF EDUCATION

County offices of education operate their own educational programs, such as schools, juvenile halls, regional occupation centers providing job-related training, special education classes and schools for students with disabilities, and environmental education schools. In addition, county offices provide administrative and supportive services to small local school districts.

About 10% of students receive special education services. The most common services are for learning disabilities such as dyslexia.

The county superintendent of schools is the chief executive officer of a county office of education. County offices of education have their own school boards, which serve as the appeal agency for local school district expulsions, territory transfers between local school districts, and charter school requests. The superintendent serves as secretary of the county board of education, which is the policymaking body for the county office and serves as the governing board for all educational programs operated at the county level. The Constitution provides for a superintendent of schools in each county; voters determine whether the superintendent is elected or appointed.

LOCAL SCHOOL DISTRICTS

Local school districts are configured in three different grade spans, although the Legislature encourages the formation of unified school districts. There were 1,028 school districts in 2013–14 (excluding special districts for specific groups):

- elementary: 531 districts
- high school: 77 districts
- unified (grades K–12): 341 districts
- other (special districts for specific groups): 79

All districts provide for an elected governing board of three to seven members serving four-year terms. School board vacancies are filled by special election or by appointment depending on the rules of the district. Many school board members serve without pay but are reimbursed for expenses. Some districts have chosen to set salaries for board members.

The school board sets local educational policies within the limits of state law, and determines the curriculum. It adopts a budget and authorizes operating and capital expenditures. The school board is responsible for meeting federal desegregation guidelines in its schools by reassigning students, establishing magnet schools, or other means.

The school board selects the superintendent, who may be a professional educator or leader from another field, to serve as administrative officer of the school district. The term of the contract is determined by the board.

If you want more information...

An excellent source for information and statistics about California's school districts is the Ed Data Website at <www.ed-data.org>.

TEACHERS

Over 296,000 full credentialed teachers taught in California public schools in 2014–15. Licenses or credentials are required for teachers in grades K–12 and are issued by the Commission on Teacher Credentialing, an independent body. In addition to this primary responsibility, the commission approves teacher preparation programs in colleges and universities and has the authority to revoke credentials.

Teachers are given tenure (permanent status) after two consecutive years of satisfactory service followed by selection for employment for the third year. A probationary teacher may be dismissed without cause. A permanent teacher may be dismissed only on specific charges of incompetency, immoral or unprofessional conduct, or conviction of a felony or crime involving moral turpitude. After being notified of charges, a teacher may request a hearing before the Commission on Professional Competence. If dismissal is ordered, the teacher may appeal to the courts.

TESTING

The state system of testing students is undergoing major changes. A report on the state superintendent's recommendation for these changes can be found at <www.cde.ca.gov/ta/tg/sa/documents/suptrecrptjan13.pdf>.

The California Department of Education Web site will offer continuing coverage of changes as they are accepted and implemented.

SCHOOL CALENDAR

Schools must be in session at least 180 days a year, but in 2008, as the state's economy deteriorated, the state gave districts permission to reduce the calendar to 175 days. By 2010 several school districts had reduced the number of days their schools were open. Because of the passage of Proposition 30 in 2012, which increased school funding, many districts which had cut school days are now adding them back. Districts must return to a 180-day school year in the 2015-16 instructional year.

Schools operate anywhere from August through June, but some operate year round with students attending on a rotating basis. For more information about year-round schools, see the California Department of Education Web site <www.cde.ca.gov/ls/fa/yr/guide.asp>.

CURRICULUM

The suggested curriculum for California's K- 12 schools is described in curriculum frameworks. Frameworks are blueprints for implementing the content standards adopted by the California State Board of Education and are developed by the Curriculum Development and Supplemental Materials Commission. The current curriculum frameworks are available online at the California State Department of Education Web site, <www.cde.ca.gov/be/st/fr/>. In addition, California has ad-

---

If you want more background ...

Frameworks are based on Education Code Section 510002 which states that there is a need for a common state curriculum, but because of economic, geographic, physical, political, and social diversity in California, there is also a need to develop educational programs at the local level, "with the guidance of competent and experienced educators and citizens." The frameworks are intended to be guidelines for districts to use in developing educational programs to meet the needs and interests of their students. Curriculum frameworks are now available in the following areas:

- career technical education
- foreign language
- health
- history-social science
- mathematics
- physical education
- reading/language arts
- science
- visual and performing arts

For more information visit: <www.cde.ca.gov/ci/cr/cf/allfwks.asp>.

The curriculum frameworks also provide the basis for the development of criteria for selecting instructional materials, kindergarten through grade twelve. The state Constitution requires the State Board of Education to review and adopt textbooks, to be furnished without cost, for use in grades one through eight throughout the state. The state also subsidizes the cost of textbooks used in high schools but does not adopt high school texts. As with frameworks, the state-adopted instructional materials provide guidelines to districts in choosing instructional materials. The law states that because of the great diversity within California, the choice of textbooks and instructional materials shall be made locally. The state encourages districts to involve teachers and the local community in the selection process. Individual districts are free to use their own funds to supplement the state-supplied materials.

About 1 in 4 public school students is an English-language learner.

opted the Common Core State Standards, as have most states. For more information, see <www.cde.ca.gov/re/cc/>.

ALTERNATIVE EDUCATIONAL PROGRAMS

State law (California Education Code [EC] sections 58500 through 58512) provides that school districts may establish and maintain alternative schools and programs of choice. These sections provide a definition of alternative schools of choice, declare the purposes of alternative schools of choice, and stipulate the requirements that alternative schools of choice must meet. Among these requirements are:

- Both the teachers and the students must volunteer to be placed in these schools.
- Alternative schools of choice provide different means of attaining the objectives of regular education and of meeting students' needs. Districts are not required to have alternative schools. Some examples of these schools are middle colleges (high schools located on community college campuses) and magnet schools.
- Alternative schools and programs of choice must meet the same standards for curriculum, instruction, and student performance as traditional schools.
- The school district must annually evaluate such schools and programs.

More information can be found at <www.cde.ca.gov/sp/eo/as/asprogramsummary.asp>.

CHARTER SCHOOLS

A charter school is a public school that provides instruction in any combination of grades, kindergarten through grade 12. Parents, teachers, or community members may initiate a charter petition, which is typically presented to and approved by a local school district governing board.

Charter status frees the school from many of the state statutes and regulations that apply to school districts. It is the intent of the California Legislature under state law that charter schools operate independently from the existing school district structure as a means of accomplishing all of the following:

- improving pupil learning
- increasing learning opportunities for all pupils, with special emphasis on expanded learning experiences for pupils who are identified as academically low achieving
- encouraging the use of different and innovative teaching methods
- creating new professional opportunities for teachers, including the opportunity to be responsible for the learning program at the school site
- providing parents and pupils with expanded choices in the types of educational opportunities that are available within the public school system
- holding the schools established under this program accountable for meeting measurable pupil outcomes, and providing the schools with a method to change from rule-based to performance-based accountability systems
- providing vigorous competition within the public school system to stimulate continual improvements in all public schools

There were approximately 1,125 charter schools in the 2013-14 school year, enrolling 514,275 students.

ONLINE EDUCATION FOR K–12 STUDENTS

Many school districts offer online education options for students. The California Department of Education defines online education as *"teacher-led education that takes place over the Internet, with the teacher and student separated geographically. Students have direct interaction with the teacher of the course using electronic means, and a learning management system is used to provide a structured learning environment.*" Find out more using the California School Directory which contains information about all California public schools, private schools, nonpublic nonsectarian schools, school districts, and county offices of education. The search feature below allows users to search for educational agencies in California by county, district, name, county-district-school (CDS) code, city, zip code, type, or status: <www.cde.ca.gov/re/sd/index.asp>.

Terms Used in Online Education

Asynchronous courses are structured so that teacher-student interaction does not occur at the same time. Asynchronous communication is available 24 hours a day, seven days a week, allowing students and teachers to participate according to their own schedules. Asynchronous programs also may incorporate synchronous (real-time) communication either digitally or through telephone conversations.

Synchronous courses provide back-and-forth communication between the teacher and students who are online at the same time for class sessions. They may use a chat program or meet in a virtual location such as Second Life. Many synchronous courses also provide asynchronous communication through email or other means outside of class sessions.

Blended (or hybrid) courses provide a combination of online delivery and supervised face-to-face sessions at a physical site away from home. In blended learning, students have some control over the time, place, path, and/or pace of the online portion of their education. Some schools offer students a blended program with a portion of their courses online and other courses taught in the classroom or through regular independent study.

Learning Management Systems (LMS), sometimes called course management systems (CMS), are the technology platforms through which online courses are offered. An LMS provides software so the instructor can create and edit course content, communicate with students, administer examinations and other assessments, and provide grade books and other feedback for students. Examples include ATutor, Blackboard, Desire2Learn, CaliQity, Moodle, and others.

Massive Open Online Enrollment Courses (MOOCS) are Web-based classes designed to allow a large number of students to enroll in a course at the same time. Several universities and some private groups provide these courses. They do not normally offer credit toward high school graduation.

SPECIALIZED PROGRAMS

Although funding and policy guidelines come from the state and federal governments, the local school districts implement and administer educational programs. Some programs are designed to meet the special needs of particular students; others attempt to improve the educational environment for all students. Some of the special programs available in California schools include the following:

50% of public school children come from low-income families.

- **The Economic Impact Aid program** provides state funds to schools which are located in low income areas or have large numbers of students with poor academic skills. A federal program, ECIA Chapter I, directs funds into the same target areas. These programs emphasize instruction in the basic skills of reading, language, and mathematics and include auxiliary services such as counseling and health services

- **Federal and state bilingual education programs** are designed to accommodate the special needs of children with limited English skills.
- **The Gifted and Talented Eduation program** (GATE) provides differentiated learning opportunities within the core curriculum for children with identified high intellectual, creative, or leadership abilities. Each district's program is determined locally, within state guidelines.
- **Federal and state migrant education programs** provide services to children of migrant workers, including supplementing the regular school program with preschool, extended day programs, and summer school.

To view a list of specialized programs supported by the California Department of Education go to <www.cde.ca.gov/sp/>.

CAREER TECHNICAL EDUCATION

The mission of career technical education in California is to *"provide industry-linked programs and services that enable all individuals to reach their career goals in order to receive economic self-sufficiency, compete in the global marketplace, and contribute to California's economic prosperity."* More information about this program, which developed out of the earlier vocational education programs, can be found at <pubs.cde.ca.gov/cte/>.

ADULT EDUCATION

Adult education programs meet a wide range of educational needs and are offered by many school districts. They serve residents over the age of 18. State funding is supplemented by federal funding for many of the programs. Among the most important programs offered are:

- adult Basic and secondary academics (literacy/high school diploma)
- English as a second language (ESL)
- citizenship preparation
- adults with disabilities
- career technical education (CTE), including apprenticeships
- parenting, family, and consumer awareness
- older adults

 More information about the adult education programs offered in California can be found at <www.cde.ca.gov/sp/ae/po/>.

Personal enrichment and recreation classes may also be offered on a fee basis by a school district.

SCHOOL FINANCE

 California supports the education of more than 6 million students in kindergarten through 12th grade and the salaries of employees as well as the construction and maintenance of over 10,000 public schools. Some of the money goes to school districts as general-purpose revenue based on a set formula. The Legislature and the governor decide how much money will go to education and how it will be divided among school districts, county offices of education, and the California Department of Education.

See Figure 11.1 for the sources of educational funding

ALLOCATION OF EDUCATION FUNDING

 The Legislature established revenue limits on what each district spends on general education. The *Serrano v. Priest*

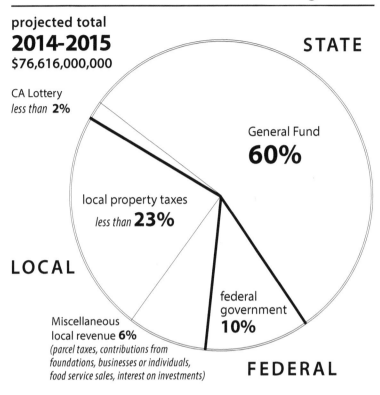

Figure 11.1 Sources of Educational Funding

projected total
2014-2015
$76,616,000,000

STATE

CA Lottery
less than **2%**

General Fund
60%

local property taxes
less than **23%**

LOCAL

Miscellaneous
local revenue **6%**
*(parcel taxes, contributions from
foundations, businesses or individuals,
food service sales, interest on investments)*

federal
government
10%

FEDERAL

data courtesy California Department of Education: <www.cde.ca.gov/fg/fr/eb/cefedbudget.asp>

court case, decided in 1976, had the effect of making districts' general-purpose money nearly equal per pupil in each type of district. Recent policy debates focused on the balance between school districts' discretionary and earmarked funding, most of which is referred to as categorical aid. Over 30 years, categorical aid increased from approximately one out of ten dollars (10.3%) received by schools statewide in 1976–77 to nearly one-third (29.9%) of statewide school revenues in 2006–07. However, a new school finance system called the Local Control Funding

Formula took effect in 2013. Full implementation of the new formula is taking place over eight years. For information on California's new school funding system, see <www.ed-data.org/article/understanding-the-local-control-funding-formula>.

Proposition 98, passed in 1988, guarantees a minimum level of funding for K–12 education, community colleges, and mental health and developmental service programs for children. Proposition 98 requires a minimum percentage of the state budget to be spent on K–14 education, guaranteeing an annual increase in education in the California budget. The actual percentage and the amount spent on education vary from year to year according to a complicated formula. As a result of Proposition 98, a minimum of 40% of California's general fund spending is mandated to be spent on education and the actual percentage of the general fund spent on education is over 50%. For more informaton: <ballotpedia.org/wiki/index.php/California_Proposition_98,_Mandatory_Education_Spending_%281988%29>.

Funding for education is one of the most complicated and controversial of all state government functions. A good source for further information on this topic is Ed Source <edsource.org/>, in addition to the California Department of Education Web site <www.cde.ca.gov/>.

POSTSECONDARY EDUCATION

74% of FTE college students in California attend public institutions (2010–2011)

Education beyond the high school level includes workplace-oriented and technical training, degree programs in the sciences and liberal arts, and postgraduate professional schools. California's public postsecondary education system is the largest in the nation, serving over 1.7 million students annually at 137 campuses throughout the state.

The California Master Plan for Higher Education established three public postsecondary systems in the state. Each system draws from a different pool of prospective students:

Figure 11.2 **Public Postsecondary Enrollment**

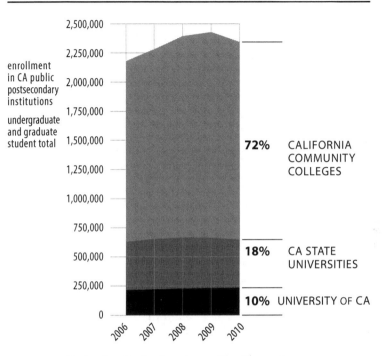

enrollment in CA public postsecondary institutions undergraduate and graduate student total

72% CALIFORNIA COMMUNITY COLLEGES

18% CA STATE UNIVERSITIES

10% UNIVERSITY OF CA

The 1849 state Constitution envisioned a university that would be of greater value to future generations than all of California's gold.

<cpec.ca.gov/StudentData/StudentSnapshot.asp?DataReport=2>

- The 10-campus University of California draws from the top eighth of each year's high school graduating class who apply on time.
- The 23-campus California State University draws from the top third, including those who are also UC-eligible.
- California's 112 community colleges, on the other hand, are open-access institutions that until recently accepted all who applied. Some have now limited acceptances because of budget cutbacks.

In fall 2010 (the most recent year for which figures are available), the three systems enrolled more than 2.3 million

Public universities provide more than one-third (⅓) of state government jobs. 2011–2012 undergraduate students, the vast majority of whom attended a community college.

The postsecondary education system in California is undergoing great changes at the present time. Sources for ongoing information about the system are available at the State Department of Education Web site <www.cde.ca.gov/> and the EdSource Web site <edsource.org/>.

Community Colleges

California's community college system is the largest such program in the country. Approximately 2.1 million students attend 112 campuses throughout the state or take courses online. Total enrollment represents one-fourth of community college enrollment nationwide. The student body is diverse in age, skill level, and academic goals; many attend part-time. Anyone over 18 years of age is eligible for admission; a high school diploma is not a prerequisite.

1.2 million FTE students in community colleges. 2011–2012

Community colleges provide students with the knowledge and background necessary to compete in today's economy. With a wide range of educational offerings, the colleges provide workforce training, basic courses in English and math, certificate and degree programs, and preparation for transfer to four-year institutions.

Unlike the University of California and California State University systems, community college districts are administered by their own locally elected boards of trustees as well as a statewide board of governors. The local boards approve curriculum and allocate funds to the programs and campuses within their jurisdictions. They also select the president of each college.

A statewide board of governors, composed of 16 members who are appointed by the governor, provides board policy guidance to the system. The board adopts regulations for all community colleges, allocates state and federal funds to districts, and reviews academic programs and construction of facilities.

The board appoints a chancellor, who is the chief administrative officer of the system.

Further information about the community college system is available on its Web site <cccco.edu>.

California State University

With 23 campuses, more than 460,000 students, and 47,000 faculty and staff, the California State University system is the largest, the most diverse, and one of the most affordable university systems in the country. The state universities emphasize undergraduate education and professional training for teachers, nurses, social workers, engineers, and many other professionals. One unit of the California State University is the California Maritime Academy in Vallejo, established to educate licensed officers and other personnel for the U.S. Merchant Marine and national maritime industries. It is the only maritime academy on the West Coast.

340,000 FTE students attend California State Universities. 2011–2012

A 25-member board of trustees is responsible for the oversight of the California State University system. The board adopts rules, regulations, and policies governing the California State University system. The board has authority over curricular development, use of property, development of facilities, and fiscal and human resources management.

Further information about the state university system is available on the Web site <calstate.edu>.

University of California

The University of California system includes more than 238,700 students and more than 198,300 faculty and staff located at ten campuses across the state. Nine of the campuses offer general educational courses, the health sciences campus is in San Francisco, and the system supports several research facilities.

The university has three roles: instruction, research, and public service. It provides undergraduate and graduate instruction

214,000 FTE students attend the various units of the University of California system. 2011–2012

in the liberal arts, sciences, and the professions, and awards doctoral degrees. It has exclusive jurisdiction in public higher education over instruction in the professions of law, medicine, dentistry, and veterinary medicine.

Besides classrooms and labs, UC has dozens of museums, concert halls, art galleries, botanical gardens, observatories, and marine centers. It offers UC Extension's continuing education courses and Cooperative Extension's agricultural advice and educational programs throughout the state.

The University of California also manages the Lawrence Berkeley National Laboratory, one of three U.S. Department of Energy national laboratories, and is involved in the Livermore and Los Alamos laboratories. These labs were established to serve U.S. defense needs; they continue today in new aspects of that mission, including response to terrorism and homeland defense.

The University of California has 10 campuses, 5 medical centers, and 3 national laboratories.

The University of California is governed by the board of regents, a 26-member board established by the California Constitution. Seven members of the board are ex officio, including the governor, lieutenant governor, speaker of the Assembly, superintendent of public instruction, and some members of the alumni associations of the University of California. A student appointed by the board, who has a vote, and two faculty members who are nonvoting members are also on the board. Other members are appointed by the governor. The board of regents appoints the president of the University of California system and its own officers: the general counsel, the treasurer, the secretary and chief of staff, and the chief compliance and audit officer.

More information about the University of California system is available on the Web site <universityofcalifornia.edu>.

FINANCING POSTSECONDARY EDUCATION

Funding for higher education in California comes from several sources:
- general fund
- federal funds
- student fees
- local taxes

Students' fees in recent years have covered a growing share of education costs. According to a report of the Legislative Analyst's Office, for 2010–11 the percentage of costs covered by the resident undergraduate fees were:

40% of UC graduates are the first in their families to go to college. 39% of those students are Pell Grant recipients.

- University of California (UC): 44 percent
- California State University (CSU): 35 percent
- California Community Colleges (CCC): 14 percent

Nearly half of all undergraduates at California's public colleges and universities receive grants or waivers that fully cover education fees. Middle-income students at UC, CSU, and CCC who do not receive grants or waivers may claim the Federal American Opportunity or Lifetime Learning tax credits.

Every year, the governor's annual budget proposal to the Legislature includes funding for the public higher education system. During the years 2008–2011, the budget allocated to higher education decreased sharply. That situation turned around somewhat as the economy improved, and the governor's proposed budget for 2015-16 includes substantial increases for the UC and CSU systems. Because the funding situation is so volatile and tax revenues uncertain, it is difficult to predict what the future will bring. Ongoing developments in funding for higher education can be tracked at the Web sites listed above for the three tiers of the system – community colleges, state universities, and the University of California. Another useful Web site is the Legislative Analyst's Office education section <lao.ca.gov/policy-areas?areaID=4>.

STATE LIBRARY

The California State Library in Sacramento is a major source of research and reference materials. It serves the people of California in several ways:

- It is the central reference and research library for state government and the Legislature.
- It provides nonpartisan research to the Legislature and the governor.
- It collects, preserves, generates, and disseminates information ranging from California's priceless historical items to today's online texts.
- It advises, consults with, and provides technical assistance to California's public libraries, and it directs state and federal funds to support local public libraries and statewide library programs and services.
- It offers special services to visually impaired and physically challenged individuals.

The Sutro Library, which features local history, the notable rare book and manuscript collections formed by Adolph Sutro, and a large genealogy collection is located on the campus of San Francisco State University in a specially designed facility in the university library. For more information: <library.sfsu.edu/about/depts/sutro.php>.

Further information about the collections and services of the California State Library can be found at its Web site <library.ca.gov/>.

The Path to Constitutional Government

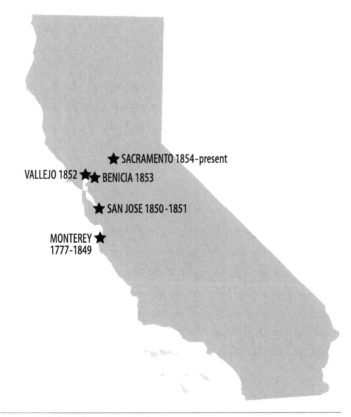

SACRAMENTO 1854-present

VALLEJO 1852

BENICIA 1853

SAN JOSE 1850-1851

MONTEREY
1777-1849

California's Capitals

The Development of *Government in California*

<www.ca.gov/about/history.html>

CHAPTER 12

As earlier chapters have shown, California government is complex and guided by a network of laws, regulations, and traditions based ultimately on the California Constitution. How did this complicated state government system develop?

EARLY GOVERNMENT STRUCTURES

California is an isolated geographic entity, separated from most of the continental United States as well as the rest of the world by a mountain range and desert areas on the east and the wide Pacific Ocean on the west. The earliest settlers were Native American groups who gradually populated the region before the arrival of Europeans. They lived in fairly small groups, each one governed by its own local rules and traditions. Exact

Figure 12.1   # Pre-1542 Language Groups

Contact between existing populations in what is now California and Europe was first established in 1542 when Portuguese explorer Juan Rodríguez Cabrillo navigated the western coast of North America. The ensuing colonization and its consequences would have dramatic and lasting effects for the tribal groups.

numbers are impossible to know, but historians estimate that before 1542 there were approximately 300,000 people living in what is now California.

Spanish explorers began visiting the western coast of North America during the 1500s, first exploring Lower (*Baja*) California and then moving up toward Upper (*Alta*) California. For 200 years, Spanish explorers continued to visit the area but they did not settle permanently. It was not until 1769 that Spain developed permanent settlements in both Upper and Lower California. Both of these areas were under the control of one governor who ruled from Loreto in Lower California. As soldiers and Franciscan missionaries moved north, local government evolved with *comandantes* given control over the military establishments (*presidios*), and priests (*padres*) given authority over the missions and towns (*pueblos*) that grew up around them.

In 1777, during the same year that English colonists on the eastern seaboard rebelled against the British king in the American Revolution, Spain moved the capital of its colony from Loreto to Monterey in recognition of Alta California's growing importance. Also that year, the first civil *pueblo* was established in San Jose and was governed by a mayor (*alcalde*) and town council. Alta California continued to grow with *presidios* at San Diego, Santa Barbara, Monterey, and San Francisco. The missions stretched along the coast from San Diego to Sonoma, and another civil *pueblo* was established in Los Angeles.

It should be noted that, beginning in the 18th century, the Russians, the British, and the French were eyeing, or —in Russia's case —actually moving down, the coast while Mexico was moving up the coast. The colonists, and later, United States officials were moving Native American tribes across the country further and further west. Today, as a consequence, there are more Native American tribes in California than in any other state, and tribes that are recognized by the U.S.

government are regarded as independent nations living within the country.

Government under Mexico

During the early 1800s, Mexicans rebelled against Spanish rule. In 1821, the country became independent, and California became a part of Mexico. Alta California had too small a population to become a province of Mexico, so it was considered a territory, which meant that local officials had less authority over local government than they would have had in a province. The capital of Alta California Territory was Monterey. After a revolt led by Juan Bautista Alvarado in 1836, the territory was transformed into a department; this gave it greater autonomy.

It was difficult to develop stable government with a population of widely scattered soldiers, priests, and independent colonists. The military *comandantes* constantly challenged the authority of the governors sent out from Mexico. Local civil disputes were settled by the *alcalde*, who was chosen locally but was replaced almost at whim. Although missions were founded with the intent of "civilizing" the Native Americans, granting them Mexican citizenship, and turning the mission towns into civil communities, this plan for secularization never proceeded on schedule. Disputes over land ownership added to the tumult and conflict that marked this period of California history. As resentment against neglect and indifference by the Mexican government grew, Californians came to think of themselves as "*Californios*" rather than Mexicans, and Mexican governors were chased out of the province with increasing frequency.

In 1846, a dispute over Texas led the United States to declare war on Mexico. Alta California was ceded to the United States in the Treaty of Guadalupe Hidalgo of 1848 that concluded the Mexican American War. The treaty provided for U.S. citizenship for Mexican Californians and upheld the validity of Mexican land grants.

Figure 12.2 Spanish & Mexican CA: 1769-1848

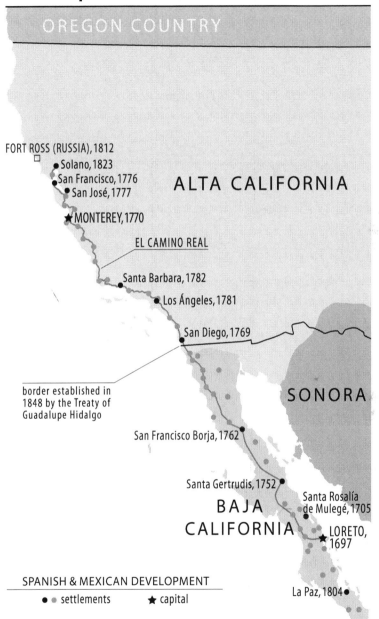

OREGON COUNTRY

FORT ROSS (RUSSIA), 1812

Solano, 1823

San Francisco, 1776

San José, 1777

ALTA CALIFORNIA

★MONTEREY, 1770

EL CAMINO REAL

Santa Barbara, 1782

Los Ángeles, 1781

San Diego, 1769

border established in 1848 by the Treaty of Guadalupe Hidalgo

SONORA

San Francisco Borja, 1762

Santa Gertrudis, 1752

Santa Rosalía de Mulegé, 1705

BAJA CALIFORNIA

LORETO, 1697

SPANISH & MEXICAN DEVELOPMENT

● ● settlements ★ capital

La Paz, 1804 ●

Much of the settlement in Alta California was by ranchers, who received land grants from the Spanish crown. The names of their ranchos are still frequently seen as place names across the state.

El Camino Real established a major route through the state that remains in heavy use, with modern highways such as the portion of U.S. Route 101 from Los Angeles to San Jose built over it.

DEVELOPING A CALIFORNIA CONSTITUTION

Many Californians would have liked the California territory to become a state, but there were disputes about whether it should be accepted into the United States as a slave state or as a free state in which slavery would be outlawed. While Congress battled to decide this issue, government in California was chaotic. In many areas there was not even the meager stability of the local *alcalde* system. When gold was discovered and immigrants poured into the area, the demand grew for a firmly established government.

First Try at a Constitution – 1849

In 1849, the military governor called for a constitutional convention to meet in Monterey in September. Of the 48 delegates, only 13 were over 40 years of age; nine were under 30. Three fourths of the men were immigrants from other states; eight of them had lived in California less than a year. In contrast, seven of the eight Spanish-surname delegates had lived in California all their lives. All were in a hurry to get their business done.

They drafted a constitution that was substantially influenced by the U.S. Constitution and those of other states. The Declaration of Rights stated that all men are free and independent and that political power is inherent in the people. It incorporated the protections of the federal Bill of Rights and forbade slavery. Suffrage was granted to male citizens. The legislature was authorized to extend the vote to Native Americans, and did so in its first session. The executive department of the government was headed by the same statewide officials as today, with the addition of a surveyor general to help resolve continuing conflicts over land ownership. Four levels of courts were established. The legislature was divided into two houses, and sessions were to be held annually. Few directions or prohibitions were imposed on the legislature, although considerable restraints were placed on corporations and banks. The legislature was to

Figure 12.3 ## Population Growth: 1849-2012

Since the U.S. took possession of California in 1848 and admitted it into the Union as a state in 1850, California has seen enormous growth from an 1850 total of nearly 250,000 inhabitants to an estimated 38,041,430 in 2012.

California is the third-largest state in the U.S. by area and the largest by population. It possesses multiple distinct regions and highly varied terrain. This size and variety, along with economic cycles, demands of industry, and availability of jobs, has led to a markedly uneven distribution of population.

FRESNO
1880: 1,112
1900: 24,892
1950: 91,669
2000: 427,652
2010: 494,665

LOS ANGELES*
1850: 1,610
1900: 102,479
1950: 1,970,358
2000: 3,694,820
2010: 3,792,621

MONTEREY**
1850: 1,872
2010: 27,810

OAKLAND
1860: 1,543
1900: 66,960
1950: 384,575
2000: 399,484
2010: 390,724

SACRAMENTO
1850: 6,820
1900: 29,282
1950: 137,572
2000: 407,018
2010: 466,488

SAN DIEGO
1850: 500
1900: 17,700
1950: 333,865
2000: 1,223,400
2010: 1,307,402

SAN FRANCISCO
1849: 25,000
1900: 342,782
1950: 775,357
2000: 776,733
2010: 805,235

SAN JOSE
1850: 3,500
1900: 21,500
1950: 95,280
2000: 894,943
2010: 945,942

*population figures for the city of Los Angeles, which is the center of a metropolitan area that in 2012 had an estimated total population of 12.8 million, the second largest in the United States and the largest in the western U.S.

**1850 population figure for Monterey County

provide for county and city government. Debt incurred by the legislature was limited to amounts under $300,000, and any debt higher than that limit required voter approval. Taxation was to be uniform in all parts of the state and assessors were to be locally elected. A wife's separate property was protected, and homesteads were protected from forced sale. All laws were to be published in both English and Spanish.

The delegates convened in September and adjourned in October. The Constitution was overwhelmingly ratified in November, with the first elected governor taking office in December 1849. The Legislature met, set up a tax system, established counties, provided for a court system, and borrowed $200,000 to get underway. The government was operating, but California was not yet a state. It was not until September 9, 1850, that Congress admitted California into the Union as the thirty-first state.

Constitution of 1879

In the 30 years between 1849 and 1879, Californians realized that the Constitution was inadequate for governing the state. There were a number of reasons for this:
- Controls over state spending were almost nonexistent.
- The powerful railroad bloc dominated government in general and the Legislature in particular.
- California's population had exploded. For every 100 persons who had been in the state in 1849, there were 1,700 by 1879.
- Many men were unemployed because of an economic depression and a drought.

Unrest was widespread. Many farmers were in revolt against railroads and other large businesses. A Workingman's Party had formed to protest imported Chinese labor, and the farmers supported the new party's effort to reform the Constitution.

In 1877, voters approved a proposal for a new Constitutional convention. The delegates to the 1878 convention worked for five months and drew up a document that became the longest of all state constitutions. They introduced changes and new provisions designed to:

- introduce severe restrictions on all branches of state government, particularly the Legislature
- reorganize the judiciary
- place restrictions on the governor's pardoning power
- make home rule charters available to cities
- make all property, tangible or intangible, subject to taxation
- regulate operations of public utilities, railroads, and other corporations
- limit the rights of Chinese people so much that the U.S. Supreme Court later found the provisions unconstitutional.

Opinion was sharply divided on the new Constitution, but it was adopted in 1879 by a solid margin. For all its detail, the new Constitution produced few of the desired reforms. These came later, as the Progressive Movement (1910–1916) gave the people a new means of reform through the initiative, referendum, recall, and direct primary. The constitution adopted in 1879— much altered over the years—is still the basis for government in California today.

Tribal Communities in California – a Special Case

More than 700,000 Native Americans live in California, about 12% of the total U.S. Native American population (2010 census) and more than in any other state. More than half of these individuals live in urban areas across the state.

Ever since California became a state, Native Americans in California have been subject to a series of conflicting policies, which have made it difficult for them to maintain their cultures and communities. During the 1850s, eighteen treaties were signed between the United States and California Native American tribes. These treaties reserved 7.5 million acres for the tribes, but the state of California persuaded the U.S.

Senate to reject the treaties. The state then passed a series of laws limiting the freedom of Native Americans to remain on land occupied by white people, authorizing the use of Native American children as slaves and indentured servants, and prohibiting Native Americans from testifying in court against a white person.

Nearly 100 years later, during the 1950s, the United States government attempted to force assimilation on all Native Americans by terminating the federal status of 44 Native American tribes in California. Many Native Americans were relocated to urban areas like Los Angeles and San Francisco. Many out-of-state Native Americans also settled in these two cities giving them the largest urban Native American population in the United States. Public Law 280, passed by Congress in 1953, transferred responsibility for the enforcement of criminal law and much civil law on tribal lands from the federal government to certain states, including California. The law did not, however, provide funding to the states to implement the law. Both Native American and non-Native American groups have expressed dissatisfaction with PL 280 over the years, but it remains substantially unchanged.

Because of this tangled history, relations between the state of California and the tribal groups and other Native Americans who live within its borders, remain complex and unsettled. Specialized health services and educational programs are available in many jurisdictions and are also offered by tribal groups. Charter schools have been established for Native American children, although few have been successful. Disparities between Native Americans and other ethnic groups remain in education, health, and justice services. Despite two hundred years of history, there is still much work to be done.

CHANGING THE CONSTITUTION

The California Constitution may be changed in three ways: amendment, constitutional convention, or revision proposed by the Legislature.

Amendment

By far the most common method of change is by amendment. The Legislature may place an amendment on the ballot by a two-thirds vote of the members of each house. The proposed amendment is placed on the ballot for voters to approve or reject. At the polls, only a simple majority of those who vote on the question is needed to pass an amendment to the Constitution.

Citizens may place a proposed amendment on the ballot as an initiative. This requires a petition of registered voters equal to eight percent of the votes cast in the last gubernatorial election.

More than 500 amendments have changed the Constitution since 1879.

Constitutional Convention

The Legislature, by a two-thirds vote of each house, may propose a convention to change the constitution. If the voters approve, the Legislature must provide for the convention within six months. California has not held a constitutional convention since 1878.

Constitutional Revision Commission

A 1962 amendment permitted the Legislature, by a vote of two-thirds of each house, to submit to the people either a partial or total revision of the constitution. A constitution revision commission, composed primarily of citizen representatives, worked for seven years to study and modernize the entire document. Ambiguities and dated language were removed and more flexibility introduced by deleting details and expressly authorizing new options. The number of words was cut in half. Three-fourths of the proposed revisions were accepted by the Legislature and the voters over a period of ten years.

The California constitution is long and complicated. It includes many regulations and details that most states leave to the Legislature. Every year, voters must decide on proposed constitutional amendments, but there has not been strong support for holding a constitutional convention and overhauling the document for fear of the changes it might bring in a delicately balanced but frequently divided political climate. For the near future, the California constitution will probably continue to grow in scope and length.

Appendix ^{PART VII}

PART VII

Abbreviations and Acronyms
The Language of Government
State Constitutional Offices
Salaries of Elected Officials
State Agencies and Departments
Regional Associations of Governments

ABBREVIATIONS AND ACRONYMS

AB	Assembly Bill
ACA	Assembly Constitutional Amendment
ACR	Assembly Concurrent Resolution
ADA	Average Daily Attendance
AFDC	Aid to Families with Dependent Children
AG	Attorney General
AJR	Assembly Joint Resolution
ALJ	Administrative Law Judge
ALRB	Agricultural Labor Relations Board
APCD	Air Pollution Control District
AQMD	Air Quality Management District
AR	Assembly Resolution
ARB	Air Resources Board
BCDC	S.F. Bay Conservation and Development Commission
BCP	Budget Change Proposal
CALCOG	California Association of Councils of Government (*See also* **COG**)
CAL/OSHA	California Occupational Safety and Health
CALHR	California State Department of Human Resources
CALPERS	California Public Employees' Retirement System
CALRECYCLE	Department of Resources, Recycling and Recovery
CALSTRS	California State Teachers' Retirement System
CALTRANS	California Department of Transportation
CCC	California Community College
CDE	California Department of Education
CEQA	California Environmental Quality Act
CHSPE	California High School Proficiency Exam
COG	Councils of Governments (*See also* **CALCOG**)
COLA	Cost of Living Adjustment
CMAQ	Congestion Mitigation and Air Quality Improvement Program
CPUC	California Public Utilities Commission

CSU	California State University
CTC	California Transportation Commission
CTE	Career Technical Education
DCA	Department of Consumer Affairs
DI	Disability Insurance
DMV	Department of Motor Vehicles
DSS	Department of Social Services
DWR	Department of Water Resources
EIR	Environmental Impact Report
FPPC	Fair Political Practices Commission
FTB	Franchise Tax Board
FTE	Full-Time-Equivalent
GAIN	Greater Avenues for Independence
GATE	Gifted and Talented Education program
GO-BIZ	Governor's Office of Economic Development
IDEA	Individuals with Disabilities Education Act
JPA	Joint Powers Agreement
K–12	Kindergarten through 12th grade
LAFCo	Local Agency Formation Commission
LMS	Learning Management Systems
LCP	Local Coastal Program
MAC	Municipal Advisory Council
MOOC	Massive Open Online Courses
MPO	Metropolitan Planning Organization
OAL	Office of Administrative Law
OPR	Office of Planning and Research
PAC	Political Action Committee
PERB	Public Employment Relations Board
PFA	Public Financing Authority

RPTA	Regional Planning Transportation Agencies
SB	Senate Bill
SBE	State Board of Education
SR	Senate Resolution
SCA	Senate Constitutional Amendment
SCR	Senate Concurrent Resolution
SCS	Sustainable Communities Strategy
SJR	Senate Joint Resolution
SSI	Supplemental Security Income
SSP	State Supplemental Payment
STP	Surface Transportation Program
STRS	State Teachers' Retirement System
TQM	Total Quality Management
UC	University of California
UI	Unemployment Insurance
ZBB	Zero-based Budgeting

THE LANGUAGE OF GOVERNMENT

Every area of special expertise has its own language, or jargon. The words and phrases may be meaningless to outsiders, but they help specialists communicate quickly and easily. In working with government sources it helps to know the language that experts use. The following list of terms used in legislative work is taken from the Legislature Information website <leginfo.ca.gov/glossary.html>.

A

ADJOURNMENT SINE DIE

Adjournment on the last day of a regular or special legislative session.

ADOPTION

Approval or acceptance of motions, amendments or resolutions.

AMENDMENT

Formal proposal to change the language of a bill after it has been introduced.

APPROPRIATION

The amount of money set aside for a specific purpose and designated from a specific source, such as the General Fund, Environmental License Plate Fund, etc.

APPROVED BY THE GOVERNOR

Signature of the governor on a bill passed by the Legislature.

ASSEMBLY

One of two houses of the California Legislature that consists of 80 members, elected for two-year terms, from districts apportioned on the basis of population.

B

BICAMERAL

A Legislature consisting of two houses.

BIENNIUM

A two-year period. This term is used to describe the two-year term of a legislature that begins in an odd-numbered year and ends in an even-numbered year.

BILL

A proposed law introduced in the Assembly or Senate and identified with a number.

BILL ANALYSIS

A document that must be prepared by committee staff prior to hearing the bill in committee. It explains how a bill would change current law and sometimes mentions support and opposition from major interest groups

BOND

A certificate of indebtedness issued by the government in return for money it has borrowed; a promise to pay a specified sum of money at a fixed time in the future and carrying interest at a fixed rate.

BOND: GENERAL OBLIGATION BONDS

Bonds for whose payment the full faith and credit of the issuing government are pledged.

BOND: REVENUE BONDS

A bond which is to be paid off by revenues produced from the facility it finances, such as user fees for a parking garage or room fees for a student dormitory.

BUDGET

A plan for expending funds by program for a given fiscal year or biennium and the means of financing the expenditures.

BUDGET: OPERATING BUDGET

A budget that applies to all expenditures other than capital expenditures for general governmental expenses.

C

CAUCUS

Conference of members of a legislative group to decide on policies or strategies; most commonly, a "party caucus" is for members of one or another political party.

CHAMBER

The Assembly or Senate meeting room where floor sessions are held.

CHAPTER

After a bill has been signed by the governor, the secretary of state assigns the bill a Chapter Number, such as Chapter 1235, Statutes of 1993, which is subsequently used to refer to the measure rather than the bill number.

COAUTHOR

Any member of either house, with the agreement of the author of a bill, may add his or her name on that member's bill as coauthor, usually indicating support for the proposal.

CODES

Bound volumes of law organized by subject matter. Law codes are also available online at <leginfo.legislature.ca.gov/faces/codes.xhtml>.

COMMITTEE

A group of legislators, usually members of the same house, assigned to consider a subject or issue and to submit a report on its recommendations for action by the body that created it. All committees are appointed by the speaker of the Assembly.

COMMITTEE REPORT

A document that a committee uses from time to time to report on matters referred to it. The document usually states findings of facts and conclusions, together with a distinct recommendation as to the disposal of the matter.

COMMITTEE: CONFERENCE COMMITTEES

Usually composed of three legislators (two from the majority party; one from the minority party) from each house who meet in public session to forge one version of similar Senate and Assembly bills. The final conference committee version must be approved by both Assembly and Senate. Assembly conferences are chosen by the speaker; Senate conferences are chosen by the Senate Rules Committee.

COMMITTEE: SPECIAL COMMITTEES

Committees that are temporary and are established either by the speaker or president by resolution or by any other legal means to consider one special subject or bill. They come to an end when they have performed the purpose for which they were established.

COMMITTEE: STANDING COMMITTEES

Committees established by the rules of the House and Senate to address particular areas such as health, transportation, or education.

COMPANION BILL

Two bills identical in wording that are introduced in each house.

CONCURRENCE

One house approving a bill as amended in the other house. If the author is unwilling to move the bill as amended by the other house, the author requests non-concurrence in the bill and asks for the formation of a conference committee.

CONCURRENT RESOLUTION

A measure introduced in one house which, if approved, must be sent to the other house for approval. The governor's signature is not required. These measures usually involve the business of the Legislature.

CONFLICT OF INTEREST

Any interest, financial or otherwise, any business or professional activity, or any obligation that is incompatible with the proper discharge of a legislator's duties in the public interest.

CONSENT CALENDAR

A group of noncontroversial bills passed by a committee or the full Assembly or Senate on one vote.

CONSTITUENT

Citizen residing within the district of a legislator.

CONSTITUTION

The written instrument embodying the fundamental principles of the state that establishes power and duties of the government and guarantees certain rights to the people.

CONSTITUTIONAL AMENDMENT

A resolution, adopted by the Legislature or presented by initiative, that affects the Constitution and requires an affirmative vote of the electorate to become effective.

D

DAILY FILE

Publication produced by the Assembly and Senate respectively for each day those houses are in session. The publication provides information about bills to be considered at upcoming committee hearings and bills eligible for consideration during the next scheduled Floor Session. Pursuant to Jt. Rule 62(a), any bill to be heard in committee must be noticed in the Daily file for four days, including weekend days. The Daily File also contains useful information about committee assignments and the legislative calendar. Daily files are available online at <www.legislature.ca.gov/port-dayfile.html>.

DAILY HISTORY

Produced by the Assembly and Senate, respectively, the day after each house has met. The History lists specific actions taken on legislation. Any measure acted upon in that house the previous day is listed in numerical order.

DAILY JOURNAL

Produced by the Assembly and Senate respectively the day after a floor session. Contains roll call votes on bills heard in policy committees and bills considered on the floor and other official action taken by the body. Any official messages from the governor are also included. A member may seek approval to publish a letter in the Journal on a specific legislative matter.

DO PASS

The affirmative recommendation made by a committee in sending a bill to the floor for final vote; do pass as amended – passage recommended providing certain changes are made.

E

EFFECTIVE DATE

The date a bill, once passed, becomes law. Unless a different date is specified, bills become law when approved.

ENACTING CLAUSE

By statutory provision, each proposed law must be preceded by the phrase "the People of the State of California do enact as follows."

ENGROSSMENT

The preparation of an exact, accurate, and official copy of a measure in the house of origin, along with amendments and proper signatures; then dispatched to the other house.

ENROLLED BILL

Whenever a bill passes both houses of the Legislature, it is ordered enrolled. In enrollment, the bill is again proofread for accuracy and then delivered to the governor. The enrolled bill contains the complete text of the bill with the dates of passage certified by the secretary of the senate and the chief clerk of the Assembly.

EXTRAORDINARY SESSION

A special legislative session called by the governor to address only those issues specified in the proclamation. They take effect immediately upon being signed by the governor.

F

FIRST READING

Each bill introduced must be read three times before the final passage. The first reading of a bill occurs when the measure is introduced.

FISCAL COMMITTEE

The Ways and Means Committee in the Assembly and the Appropriations Committee in the Senate, to which all fiscal bills are referred if they are approved by policy committees. If the fiscal committee approves a bill, it then moves to the floor.

FISCAL YEAR

The period used for budgeting and accounting.

FLOOR

The Assembly or Senate chambers.

FULL-TIME-EQUIVALENT

FTE (full-time equivalent) is a unit that indicates the workload of an employee or the course load of a student in a way that makes workloads comparable.

H

HEARING, PUBLIC

A formal session of a legislative committee, whereby interested members of the public are invited to present testimony on a proposal; distinguished from an informational briefing, which the public is usually allowed to attend but not present testimony.

HELD IN COMMITTEE

The defeat of a measure by the decision of a standing committee not to return it to the full house for further consideration.

HOUSE

Generally, either body or chamber of the Legislature. (If capitalized, it refers to the U.S. House of Representatives.)

I

INACTIVE FILE

The portion of the Daily File containing legislation that is ready for floor consideration, but, for a variety of reasons, is dead or dormant. An author may move a bill to the inactive file and subsequently move it off the inactive file at a later date. During the final weeks of the legislative session, measures may be moved there by the leadership as a method of encouraging authors to take up their bills promptly.

INITIATIVE

A method of legislating that requires a vote of the people instead of a vote of the Legislature for a measure to become law.

INTERIM

The period of time between the end of the legislative year and the beginning of the next legislative year. The legislative year ends on August 31 in even-numbered years and September 15 in odd-numbered years.

INTRODUCTION

The transmittal of a bill from a representative's or senator's office to the respective chief clerk's office for acceptance and numbering.

ITEM VETO

The governor's refusal to approve a portion or item of a bill; however, the remainder of the bill is approved.

J

JOINT COMMITTEE

A committee composed of a specified number of members of both houses.

JOURNAL

The official chronological record of the proceedings of the Senate and Assembly, certified, indexed, printed, and bound at the close of each session. <www.legislature.ca.gov/research_and_publications/publications/publications.html>

JOINT RESOLUTION

Expresses an opinion about an issue pertaining to the federal government; forwarded to Congress for its information. Requires the approval of both Assembly and Senate but does not require the signature of the governor to take effect.

L

LAW

Rule of conduct determined by the people through their elected representatives, or by direct vote.

LEGISLATIVE COUNSEL'S DIGEST

The digest is a brief summary of the changes the proposed bill would make to current law. The digest is found on the front of each printed bill.

LEGISLATIVE DEADLINES

Deadline set by a legislative body for specified action, such as bill introduction, committee action, or initial passage of bills by either house.

M
MEASURE
Any bill, resolution, or constitutional amendment that is acted upon by the Legislature.

O
ON FILE
A bill on second or third reading or unfinished business awaiting concurrence is on file; listed in the Assembly or Senate Daily File.

P
POLICY COMMITTEE
Each house of the legislature has a number of committees referred to as "policy" committees. As bills are introduced in each house, the Rules Committee assigns each to a policy committee. The policy committee sets up public hearings on the bills, conducts hearings and, following such testimony, votes on whether or not to recommend passage of the bill to the floor of the respective house. Other actions a policy committee may take include amending a bill and re-referring it to the same or another committee for additional hearings.

PRESIDENT OF THE SENATE
The state Constitution designates the lieutenant governor as president of the Senate, allowing him to preside over the Senate and cast a vote only in the event of a 20–20 tie. The lt. governor's role is largely ceremonial because he has not cast a tie-breaking vote since 1975 and, in practice, does not preside over the Senate.

Q
QUORUM
The number of members of a house, committee, or other group that must be present before the group may conduct official business.

QUORUM CALL
Transmitting the message that members are needed to establish a quorum so proceedings can begin.

R
READING
Presentation of a bill before either house by the reading of the

title thereof; a stage in the enactment of a measure. A bill, until passed, is either in process of first, second or third reading, no matter how many times it has actually been read.

REAPPORTIONMENT
Redistricting the state for elections; completed every ten years following the national census.

RECONSIDERATION
The act of requesting the return of a measure sent to the second house or to the governor, but not yet enacted into law, for the purpose of reconsidering the action taken on that measure.

REFERENDUM
The principle or practice of submitting a law to popular vote after the filing of a petition expressing the wish of the people to vote on such law.

REFERRAL
The sending or referring of a measure to a committee or committees.

REPORTING OUT
Action by a committee on a measure, which moves the measure out of the committee.

RESOLUTION
An opinion, expressed by one or both houses, that does not have the force of law. Concurrent resolutions are voted on by both houses but do not require the governor's signature; joint resolutions are voted on by both houses

RESOLUTION: MEMORIAL RESOLUTION
A non-substantive resolution used to convey the sympathy and condolences of the Legislature on the passing of a constituent or a dignitary.

ROLL CALL
A vote of a committee or the full Assembly or Senate. Committee roll calls are conducted by the committee secretary, who calls each member's name in alphabetical order with the Chair's name last. Assembly roll calls are conducted electronically with each member pushing a button from his/her assigned seat. Senate roll calls are conducted by the Reading Clerk, who reads each senator's name in alphabetical order.

S

SECOND READING
Each bill introduced must be read three times before final

passage. Second reading occurs after a bill has been reported from committee.

SECTION

Portion of the codes, cited in each bill, which proposes to amend, create, or replace same.

SENATE

One of two houses of the California Legislature that consists of 40 members elected from districts apportioned on the basis of population, one-half of whom are elected or re-elected every two years for four-year terms.

SESSION

Period during which the Legislature meets: Regular – the biennial session at which all classes of legislation may be considered; Extraordinary – special session, called by, and limited to matters specified by the governor; Daily – each day's meeting; Joint – meeting of the two houses together.

SPEAKER

Highest ranking member of the Assembly; elected by all Assembly members at the beginning of each two-year legislative session. Presides over the Assembly.

STATUTES

Compilation of all enacted bills, chaptered by the secretary of state in the order in which they became law, and prepared in book form by the state printer.

SUNSET LAW

A provision shutting off a program or agency on a specific date, requiring reexamination and a fresh authorization prior to that date to continue.

T

THIRD READING

Each bill introduced must be read three times before final passage. Third reading occurs when the measure is about to be taken up on the floor of either house for final passage.

THIRD READING ANALYSIS

A summary of a measure ready for floor consideration. Contains most recent amendments and information regarding how members voted on the measure when it was heard in committees. Senate floor analyses also list support or opposition information on interest groups and government agencies.

TITLE
> A brief italicized paragraph identifying the subject matter, and preceding the contents, of a measure.

U

UNFINISHED BUSINESS
> That portion of the Daily File that contains measures awaiting Senate or Assembly concurrence with amendments taken in the other house. Also contains measures vetoed by the governor for a 60-day period after the veto. The house where the vetoed bill originated has 60 days to attempt to override.

URGENCY
> An urgency measure goes into effect immediately once passed by both houses and signed by the governor. This type of measure requires a 2/3 vote.

V

VETO
> A power vested in the governor to prevent the enactment of measures passed by the Legislature, by returning them, with objections, to the Legislature.

VOTE
> There are two categories of votes: majority and two-thirds.

VOTE: MAJORITY VOTE
> A vote of more than half of the legislative body considering a measure. The full Assembly requires a majority vote of 41 and the full Senate requires 21, based on their memberships of 80 and 40 respectively.

VOTE: TWO-THIRDS (2/3) VOTE
> A vote of at least 2/3 of the legislative body considering a measure. The full Assembly requires a 2/3 vote of 54 and the full Senate requires 27, based on their memberships of 80 and 40 respectively.

SOME ADDITIONAL GOVERNMENT GLOSSARIES:
California State Legislature <www.legislature.ca.gov/quicklinks/glossary.html>
Superior Court of California Legal Glossary <saccourt.ca.gov/general/legal-glossaries/docs/english-legal-glossary.pdf>
California State Senate Glossary <senate.ca.gov/glossary/>

STATE CONSTITUTIONAL OFFICES

GOVERNOR
Edmund G. Brown Jr.
State Capitol, Suite 1173 Sacramento, CA 95814
Telephone: (916) 445-2841
Web site: www.gov.ca.gov
Twitter: @JerryBrownGov

LIEUTENANT GOVERNOR
Gavin Newsom
State Capitol, Room 1114, Sacramento, CA 95814
Telephone: (916) 445-8994
Web site: www.ltg.ca.gov
Twitter: @GavinNewsom

SECRETARY OF STATE
Alex Padilla
1500 11th Street, Sacramento, CA 95814
Telephone: (916) 653-6814
Web site: www.sos.ca.gov
Email: secretary.padilla@sos.ca.gov
Twitter: @sosnews

ATTORNEY GENERAL
Kamala D. Harris
DEPARTMENT OF JUSTICE
1300 "I" Street, Sacramento, CA 95814
Mailing Address: P.O. Box 944255, Sacramento, CA 94244-2550
Telephone: (916) 445-9555
Web site: www.oag.ca.gov
Email: piu@doj.ca.gov
Twitter: @CalAGHarris

STATE CONTROLLER
Betty T. Yee
300 Capitol Mall, Suite 1850, Sacramento, CA 95814
Mailing Address: P.O. Box 942850, Sacramento, CA 94250

Telephone: (916) 445-2636
Web site: www.sco.ca.gov
Twitter: @CAController

STATE TREASURER

John Chiang
915 Capitol Mall, Room 110, Sacramento, CA 95814
Mailing Address: P.O. Box 942809, Sacramento, CA 94209-0001
Telephone: (916) 653-2995
Web site: www.treasurer.ca.gov
Twitter: @CalTreasurer

INSURANCE COMMISSIONER

Dave Jones
DEPARTMENT OF INSURANCE
300 Capitol Mall, Suite 1700, Sacramento, CA 95814
Telephone: (916) 492-3500
Consumer Hotline: 1-800-927-HELP (4357) or
(213) 897-8921 (outside CA)
Web site: www.insurance.ca.gov
Twitter: @CDInews

STATE SUPERINTENDENT OF PUBLIC INSTRUCTION

Tom Torlakson
DEPARTMENT OF EDUCATION
1430 N Street, Sacramento, CA 95814
Mailing Address: 1430 N Street, Suite 5602, Sacramento,
CA 95814
Telephone: (916) 319-0800
Web site: www.cde.ca.gov
Email: superintendent@cde.ca.gov
Twitter: @CADeptEd

STATE BOARD OF EQUALIZATION

Cynthia Bridges Executive Director
450 N Street, MIC 73, Sacramento, CA 95814
Mailing Address: P.O. Box 942879, Sacramento, CA 94279
Telephone: (916) 327-4975
Web site: www.boe.ca.gov
Twitter: @CA_BOE_News

SALARIES of ELECTED OFFICIALS

Proposition 112, passed by voters in June 1990, established the commission to set the salaries and benefits of members of the Legislature and the state's other elected officials.

Proposition 1F, passed by voters in May 2009, prevents the commission from increasing elected officials' salaries during budget deficit years.

For more information, go to the California Citizens Compensation Commission website <calhr.ca.gov/cccc/Pages/home.aspx>.

Current Salaries (effective December 1, 2014)
Governor $177,467
Lieutenant Governor $133,100
Attorney General $154,150
Controller $141,973
Treasurer $141,973
Secretary of State $133,100
Superintendent of Public Instruction $154,150
Insurance Commissioner $141,973
Member, Board of Equalization $133,100
Members, State Legislature $97,197
Assembly Speaker/Senate President Pro Tem $111,776
Minority Floor Leader $111,776
Majority Floor Leader $104,486
Second Ranking Minority Leader $104,486

SALARIES OF ELECTED OFFICIALS 2012–2013

Current salaries (effective December 3, 2012–December 3, 2013)
Salaries were reduced by 5% from the previous period.
Governor $165,288
Lieutenant Governor $123,965
Attorney General $143,571
Secretary of State $123,965
Controller $132,230

Past Salaries Of Elected Officials, 2012–2013   /cont'd ...

Treasurer $132,230
Superintendent of Public Instruction $143,571
Insurance Commissioner $132,230
Members, Board of Equalization $123,965
Speaker of the Assembly $104,105
President Pro Tem of the Senate $104,105
Minority Floor Leader $104,105
Majority Floor Leader $97,315
Second Ranking Minority Leader $97,315
All Other Legislators $90,526

Past Salaries Of Elected Officials, 2011–2012

Governor $173,987
Lieutenant Governor $130,490
Attorney General $151,127
Secretary of State $130,490
Controller $139,189
Treasurer $139,189
Superintendent of Public Instruction $151,127
Insurance Commissioner $139,189
Members, Board of Equalization $130,490
Speaker of the Assembly $109,584
President Pro Tem of the Senate $109,584
Minority Floor Leader $109,584
Majority Floor Leader $102,437
Second Ranking Minority Leader $102,437
All Other Legislators $95,291

STATE AGENCIES and DEPARTMENTS

In 2010, Governor Jerry Brown began a reorganization of the state's agencies and departments. This reorganization is scheduled to go into effect in July 2013. Following are most of the agencies and the departments under their direction. Please visit these Web sites for current information or check with the district office of your state legislators for assistance.

THE GOVERNMENT OPERATIONS AGENCY
Departments that are involved in running the enterprise of state government, providing a single focus on state services:

Department of General Services   www.dgs.ca.gov

Department of Human Resources   www.calhr.ca.gov

Department of Technology   www.otech.ca.gov

Office of Administrative Law   www.oal.ca.gov

Public Employees' Retirement System   www.calpers.ca.gov

State Teachers' Retirement System   www.calstrs.com

State Personnel Board   www.spb.ca.gov

Victims Compensation and
Government Claims Board   www.vcgcb.ca.gov

Franchise Tax Board   www.ftb.ca.gov

TRANSPORTATION AGENCY

<calsta.ca.gov>
includes the following departments:

Transportation   www.dot.ca.gov

Motor Vehicles   www.dmv.ca.gov

High-Speed Rail Authority   www.hsr.ca.gov

Highway Patrol   www.chp.ca.gov

Transportation Commission   www.catc.ca.gov

Board of Pilot Commissioners   www.bopc.ca.gov

Office of Traffic Safety   www.ots.ca.gov

BUSINESS, CONSUMER SERVICE AND HOUSING AGENCY

<bcsh.ca.gov>
Business and consumer-related departments that regulate or license industries, business activities, or professionals, including:

Consumer Affairs   www.dca.ca.gov

Housing and Community Development   www.hcd.ca.gov

Fair Employment and Housing   www.dfeh.ca.gov

Alcoholic Beverage Control   www.abc.ca.gov

Horse Racing Board   www.chrb.ca.gov

Seismic Safety Commission   www.seismic.ca.gov

Business Oversight   www.dbo.ca.gov

Housing Finance Agency   <calhfa.ca.gov>

HEALTH AND HUMAN SERVICES AGENCY
Department of Aging
<www.aging.ca.gov>

Child Support Services   www.childsup.ca.gov

Community Services and Development
www.csd.ca.gov

Developmental Services   www.dds.ca.gov

Emergency Medical Services Authority   www.emsa.ca.gov

Health Care Services   www.dhcs.ca.gov

Managed Risk Medical Insurance Board   www.mrmib.ca.gov

State Hospitals   www.dsh.ca.gov

Rehabilitation   www.rehab.cahwnet.gov

Social Services   www.cdss.ca.gov

Office of Statewide Health Planning and Development
www.oshpd.ca.gov

Public Health   www.cdph.ca.gov

Food and Agriculture   www.cdfa.ca.gov

Veterans Affairs   www.calvet.ca.gov

LABOR AND WORKFORCE DEVELOPMENT AGENCY
<labor.ca.gov>

Public Employees Retirement Board   www.calpers.ca.gov

Public Employment Relations Board   www.perb.ca.gov

Agricultural Labor Relations Board   www.alrb.ca.gov

Employment Development Department   www.edd.ca.gov

Department of Industrial Relations   www.dir.ca.gov

Workforce Investment Board   www.cwib.ca.gov

Unemployment Insurance Appeals Board   <cuiab.ca.gov>

Employment Training Panel   <www.etp.ca.gov>

CALIFORNIA ENVIRONMENTAL PROTECTION AGENCY
<calepa.ca.gov>

Department of Resources, Recycling and Recovery
www.calrecycle.ca.gov

Air Resources Board   www.arb.ca.gov

Department of Pesticide Regulation   www.cdpr.ca.gov

Department of Toxic Substances Control   www.dtsc.ca.gov

Office of Environmental Health Hazard Assessment
www.oehha.ca.gov

State Water Resources Control Board   www.waterboards.ca.gov

NATURAL RESOURCES AGENCY

California Coast Commission   www.coastal.ca.gov

Tahoe Conservancy   www.tahoe.ca.gov

Santa Monica Mountains Conservancy   www.smmc.ca.gov

Sacramento-San Joaquin Delta Conservancy
www.deltaconservancy.ca.gov

Colorado River Board of California   www.crb.ca.gov

Department of Conservation   www.conservation.ca.gov

California Conservation Corps   www.ccc.ca.gov

California Energy Commission   www.energy.ca.gov

Department of Fish and Game   www.wildlife.ca.gov

Department of Forestry and Fire Protection   www.calfire.ca.gov

Department of Parks and Recreation   www.parks.ca.gov

Department of Water Resources   www.water.ca.gov

Delta Stewardship Council   www.deltacouncil.ca.gov

Exposition Park   www.expositionpark.org

DEPARTMENT OF CORRECTIONS AND REHABILITATION
<www.cdcr.ca.gov>

Adult Operations Division   www.cdcr.ca.gov/Adult_Operations/

Juvenile Justice Division   www.cdcr.ca.gov/juvenile_justice/

Board of State and Community Corrections   www.bscc.ca.gov

Board of Juvenile Parole Hearings
www.cdcr.ca.gov/Juvenile_Justice/Juvenile_Parole_Board/

Adult Board of Parole Hearings   www.cdcr.ca.gov/parole/

REGIONAL ASSOCIATIONS of GOVERNMENTS

ASSOCIATION OF BAY AREA GOVERNMENTS
101 - 8th Street, Oakland CA 94607
Mailing Address: P.O. BOX 2050 Oakland, CA 94604-2050
Tel 510.464.7900
Web site <abag.ca.gov>

ASSOCIATION OF MONTEREY BAY AREA GOVERNMENTS
445 Reservation Road, Suite G, Marina, CA 93933.
Tel 831.883.3750
Web site <ambag.org>

BUTTE COUNTY ASSOCIATION OF GOVERNMENTS
2580 Sierra Sunrise Terrace, Suite 100, Chico, CA 95928-8441
Tel 530.879.2468
Web site <bcag.org>

CALAVERAS COUNCIL OF GOVERNMENTS
444 E. Saint Charles Street/Highway 49, San Andreas, CA 95249
Mailing Address: P. O. Box 280, San Andreas, CA 95249
Tel 209.754.2094
Web site <calacog.org>

CALIFORNIA ASSOCIATION OF COUNCILS OF GOVERNMENTS
1100 K Street Suite 101
Sacramento, CA 95814
Tel 916.557.1170
Web site <calacog.org>

FRESNO COUNCIL OF GOVERNMENTS
2035 Tulare Street, Suite 201, Fresno, CA 93721
Tel 559.233.4148
Web site <fresnocog.org>

HUMBOLDT COUNTY ASSOCIATION OF GOVERNMENTS
611 I Street, Suite B, Eureka, CA 95501
Tel 707.444.8208
Web site <hcaog.net>

KERN COUNCIL OF GOVERNMENTS
1401 19th Street, Suite 300, Bakersfield, CA 93301
Tel 661.861.2191
Web site <kerncog.org>

KINGS COUNTY ASSOCIATION OF GOVERNMENTS
339 West D Street, Suite B, Lemoore, CA 93245
Tel 559.852.2654
Web site <kingscog.org>

LAKE COUNTY/CITY AREA PLANNING COUNCIL
367 N. State Street, Suite. 206, Ukiah, CA 95482
Tel 707.263.7799
Web site <lakeapc.org>

MENDOCINO COUNCIL OF GOVERNMENTS
367 N. State Street, Suite 206, Ukiah, CA 95482
Tel 707.463.1859
Web site <mendocinocog.org>

MERCED COUNTY ASSOCIATION OF GOVERNMENTS (MCAG)
369 West 18th Street, Merced, CA 95340
Tel 209.723.3153
Web site <mcagov.org>

SACRAMENTO AREA COUNCIL OF GOVERNMENTS
1415 L Street, Sacramento, CA, 95814
Tel 916.321.9000
Web site <sacog.org>

SAN DIEGO ASSOCIATION OF GOVERNMENTS
401 B Street, Suite 800, San Diego, California 92101
Tel 619.699.1900
Web site <sandag.org>

SAN LUIS OBISPO COUNCIL OF GOVERNMENTS
1114 Marsh Street, San Luis Obispo, CA 93401
Tel 805.781.4219
Web site <slocog.org>

SAN JOAQUIN COUNCIL OF GOVERNMENTS
555 E. Weber Avenue, Stockton, CA 95202-2804
Tel 209.235.0600
Web site <sjcog.org>

SANTA BARBARA COUNTY ASSOCIATION OF GOVERNMENTS
260 North San Antonio Road, Suite B, Santa Barbara, CA, 93110
Tel 805.961.8900
Web site <sbcag.org/>

SOUTHERN CALIFORNIA ASSOCIATION OF GOVERNMENTS
818 West 7th Street, 12th Floor, Los Angeles, CA 90017
Tel 213.236.1800
Web site <scag.ca.gov>

STANISLAUS COUNCIL OF GOVERNMENTS
111 I Street, Suite 308, Modesto, CA 95354
Tel 209.525.4600
Web site <stancog.org>

TAHOE METROPOLITAN PLANNING ORGANIZATION
128 Market Street, Suite F, Stateline, NV 89449
Tel 775.588.4547
Web site <tahoempo.org/>

TULARE COUNTY ASSOCIATION OF GOVERNMENTS
210 N. Church Street, Suite B, Visalia, CA 93291
Tel 559.623-0450
Web site <tularecog.org/>

WESTERN RIVERSIDE COUNCIL OF GOVERNMENTS
4080 Lemon Street, 3rd floor, MS 1032, Riverside, CA 92501
Tel 950.955.7985
Web site <wrcog.cog.ca.us>

INDEX

COLOPHON

We wanted to use typefaces designed in or reflective of California. We chose to use two Adobe type families.

The text face is Chaparral Pro, designed by Carol Twombly for Adobe and released in 2000. This typeface combines the legibility of slab serif designs popularized in the 19th century with the grace of 16th-century roman book lettering, giving it an accessible and friendly appearance. Like the drought-resistant brush that blooms on the arid coastal range near Twombly's California home, Chaparral's highly functional design is surprisingly beautiful.

Chaparral is a biome characterized by hot dry summers and cool moist winters and dominated by a dense growth of mostly small-leaved evergreen shrubs, as that found in the foothills of California.

The display face is Myriad Pro, designed by Carol Twombly and Robert Slimbach of Adobe and was first released in 1992. Myriad has a warmth and readability that result from the humanistic treatment of letter proportions and design detail.

Made in the USA
San Bernardino, CA
10 January 2020